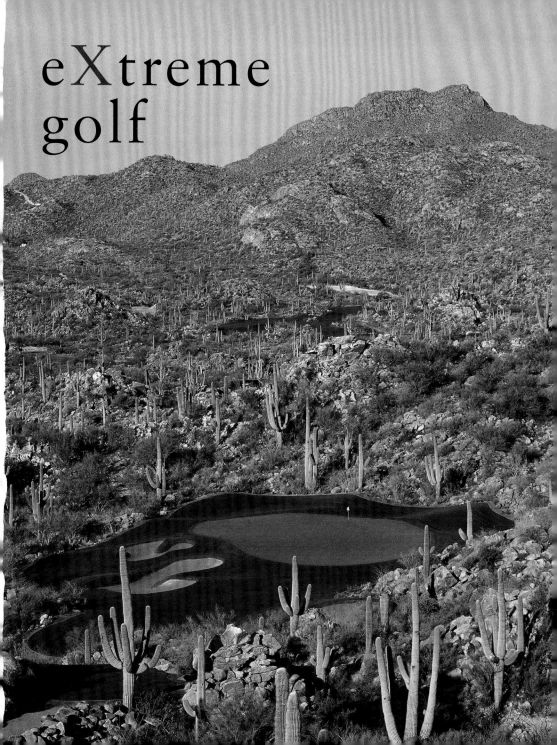

eXtreme
golf

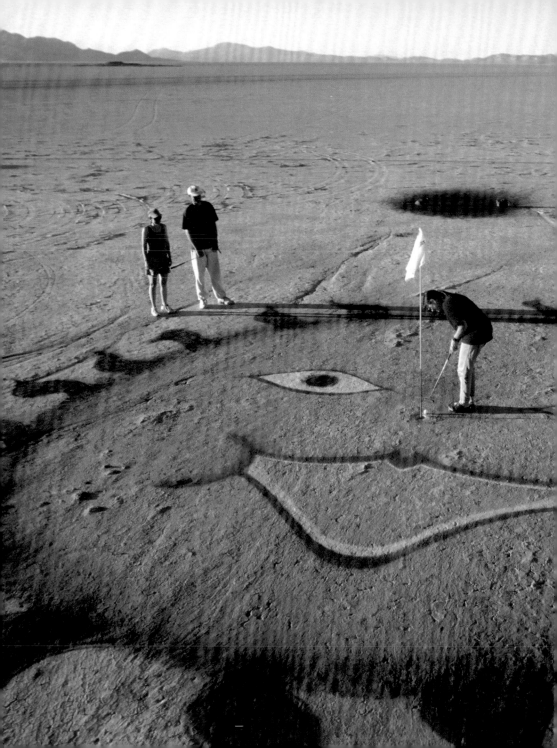

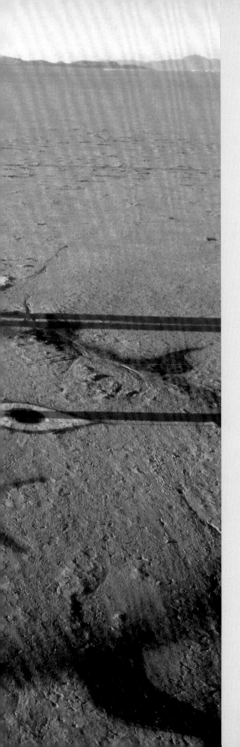

eXtreme golf

the world's most unusual, fantastic and bizarre courses

duncan lennard

PAVILION

First published in Great Britain in 2004 by
PAVILION

An imprint of the Anova Book Company Ltd
151 Freston Road, London W10 6TH

This reduced format edition published in 2006

Text © Duncan Lennard 2004

Design and layout © Pavilion 2004

For picture acknowledgements see page 160

Map artwork on pages 6-7 by Hardlines Ltd

The moral right of the author has been asserted

Design: Martin Hendry
Commissioning Editor: Nina Sharman
Editor: Katherine Morton
Picture Research: Jamie Dikomite

A CIP catalogue record for this book is available
from the British Library.

ISBN: 1 86205 725 7

Colour reproduction by Classic Scan, Singapore
Printed and bound by SNP Leefung, China

10 9 8 7 6 5 4 3 2 1

www.anovabooks.com

Contents

Y

Extreme Golf on the Map

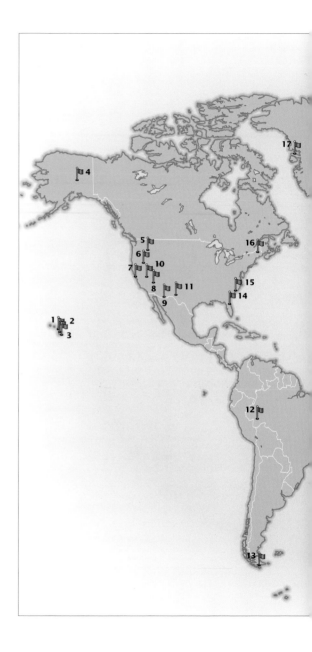

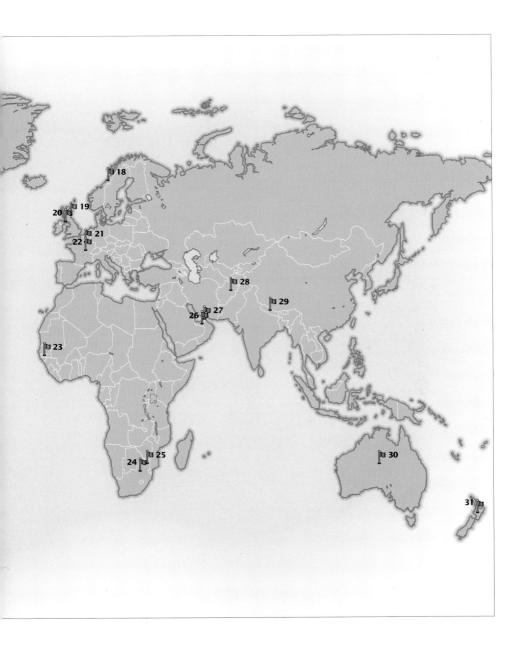

Introduction

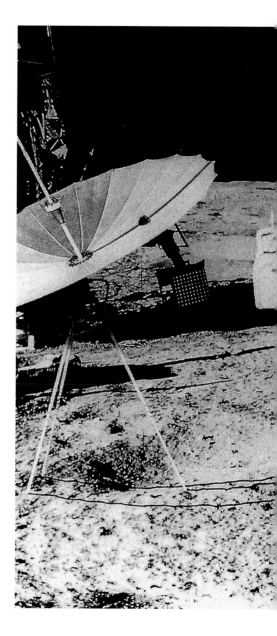

GOLFERS TEND TO exaggerate how far they can hit the ball. So when the American astronaut Alan Shepard told us that the 6-iron shot he struck from the surface of the moon flew "for miles and miles and miles", it was wise to take it with a pinch of moondust. In fact, a shot hit 200 yards (201m) on earth would travel about 1,200 yards (1,097m) on the moon. Allowing for Shepard's restrictive space suit and backpack, his moon shot probably travelled no more than 600 yards (549m).

It's no surprise that man has seen fit to leave this planet in search of a new extreme golf challenge. Think of any landscape on earth, and you can rest assured someone has already placed a tee marker at one end of it and a small hole at the other. Perhaps you fancy playing a 702-yard (642m) par-6 across a scorched and scorpion-ridden desert floor? Head for Lucifer's Anvil Golf Course in Nevada, USA, and there it is. How about a tough par-4 through a war zone, with tanks and bomb craters for hazards? Try the 1st hole at the Qargha Lakes course in Kabul, Afghanistan. You can golf under an active volcano at The Waikoloa Resort in Hawaii; or on an ice-munching glacier during the Drambuie World Ice Golf Championship in Greenland. If that sounds a bit chilly for your tastes, you might prefer to smash a ball up and

▶ **Over the moon**
When 15-handicapper Alan Shepard struck three 6-irons from the surface of the moon in February 1971, he completed extreme golf's extraordinary 500-year journey from the North Sea to the Sea of Tranquility.

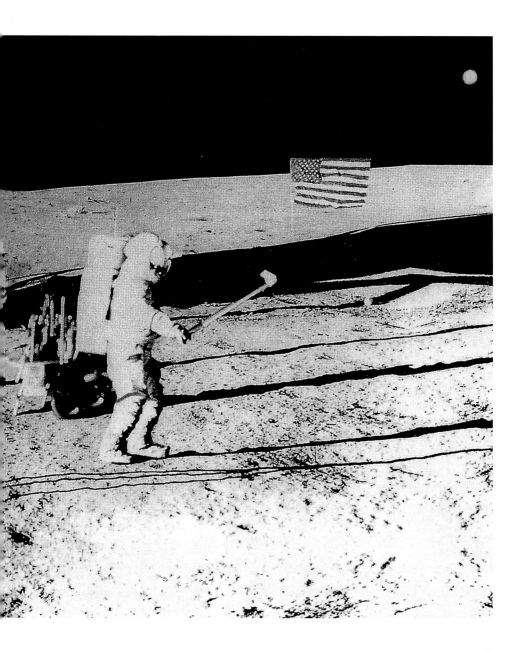

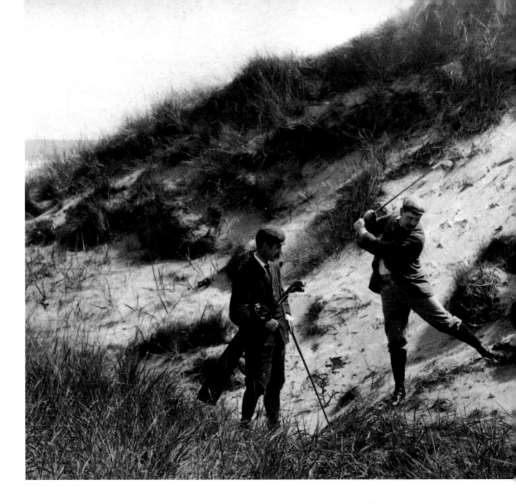

down the mountains of America at The UX Open Challenge. You can even play past lions, elephants, giraffes and water buffalo at the Hans Merensky resort, next door to South Africa's famed Kruger National Park.

Our quest to take the game of golf into ever more exotic environments has seen courses spring up in all corners of the world – and in the unlikeliest locations. There is a course 300 miles (483km) inside the Arctic Circle at North Cape,

Norway, where you can golf under the midnight sun for six months of the year and under the aurora borealis for the other six. Almost 11,000 miles (17,699km) from there is the world's southernmost course – Ushuaia in Argentina, which is incessantly strafed by gales from the infamous Drake Passage. Australia surely has the world's hottest course: Alice Springs, in the country's red centre, regularly experiences temperatures above 50˚C (122˚F). And if you want

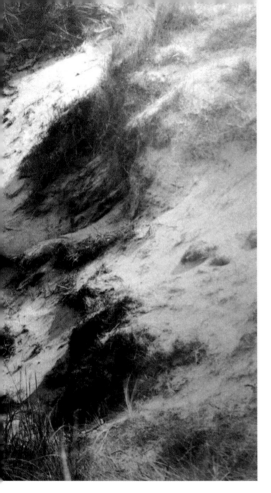

◀ **Warriors of the wasteland**

*The golfer's appetite for playing in extreme conditions dates
back to the sport's genesis. Golf was born in the fifteenth
century among the dunes of Scotland's coastline, played on
wasteland no-one else could find a use for.*

floating green for the par-3 14th. At Macon la Salle
Golf Club, France, the curvaceous fairways are
designed to represent the naked body.

These are just some of the remarkable courses
featured in this book. That people the world over
queue up to play them suggests that for golfers, a
hole can never be too weird – nor too tough.
Perhaps there is a logic in this somewhere: golf is
arguably the world's most difficult game, and by
definition attracts those with a masochistic streak.
We'll deny it of course, but the harder it gets, the
more we like it.

Not only is golf a game played by lovers of
vibrant vistas, but any player will tell you that the
higher the stakes, the more satisfying it is to hit a
successful shot. Ask the members at Rotorua Golf
Club, New Zealand, which hole they prefer – the
14th, played across an egg-reeking, sulphurous
steam-pit fed by the bowels of the earth; or the
5th, played along a manicured stretch of fairway?
They'll say the 14th every time. Given the golfer's
astonishing determination to play outrageous golf
holes, it seems only par for the course that Alan
Shepard prepared for the Apollo XIV mission of
1971 by fashioning a makeshift 6-iron out of three
bits of aluminium, an axe handle and some Teflon.

The courses in this book span the blue globe
Shepard would have seen had he forgotten his golf
lessons and lifted his head. They may not rival the
view from the Fra Mauro uplands, but you will end
up wanting to play them all. It's the only way to
make your extreme golf experience complete.

to play golf on the moon but don't fancy the
572,000-mile (920,348km) round trip, consider
teeing up on the lunar terrain of La Paz Golf Club,
Bolivia – the world's highest course at 2 miles
(3.2km) above sea level.

Even traditional courses have found ways to
make their challenge extraordinary. At the home of
golf itself, St Andrews in Scotland, they discovered
they could intensify the test by playing the course
backwards. At Coeur d'Alene, Idaho, they built a

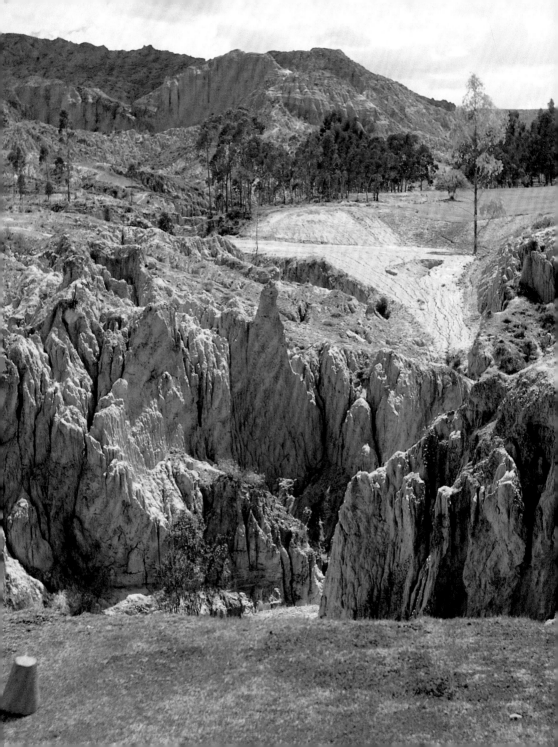

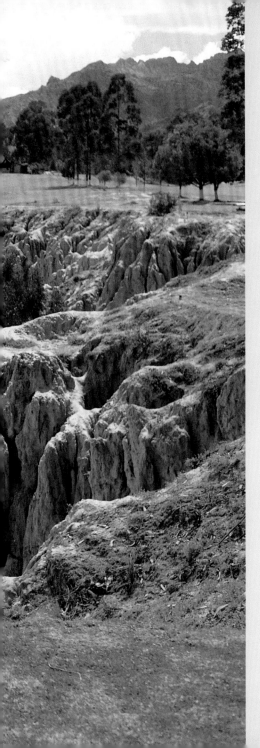

Location Location Location

A sandstone moonscape dominates the scene at Bolivia's La Paz Golf Club, the world's highest course, at 2 miles (3.2km) above sea level. The world's golf courses can take you below sea level also, or to the very fringes of the Arctic and Antarctic. If you prefer your golf a little warmer you can also play in stifling heat at Alice Springs in Australia, the world's hottest course.

Awesome Eight Golf Challenge

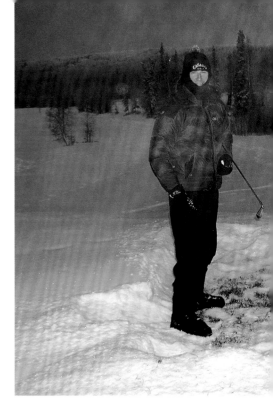

TAKING GOLF TO THE EXTREME

Nobody said golf was meant to be easy. You will not have experienced the game's ultimate challenge, however, until you have played in the harshest conditions the planet can throw at you. Cue the Awesome Eight Golf Challenge, an event that calls for energy, endurance, enthusiasm and a little bit of cash. To complete the challenge you must play eight of the world's most extreme golf courses in one year. There are just two conditions: you are not allowed to use a caddie, a trolley or a buggy; and you must carry your clubs. If you succeed, you will earn a certificate and become a member of the

Awesome Eight Golf Society, surely the most exclusive golf society in the world.

The concept of the Awesome Eight was dreamed up by Robin Sieger, a motivational speaker and self-taught extreme athlete. "The idea was to create an endurance or extreme challenge for golfers along the lines of the Seven Summits Mountaineering Challenge, which takes in the highest peak on each of the seven continents. It's for a particular type of golfer who has an adventurous soul and wants to challenge himself, but who does not want to sail an ocean or climb a mountain. Of course, you don't have to do all eight in one go, so it gives you a bit more flexibility to achieve your goal."

THE AWESOME COURSES

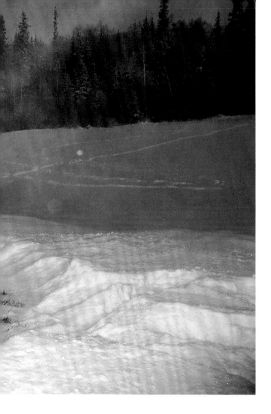

"It's for a particular type of golfer who has an adventurous soul and wants to challenge himself, but who does not want to sail an ocean or climb a mountain. Of course, you don't have to do all eight in one go, so it gives you a bit more flexibility to achieve your goal."

ROBIN SIEGER

◀ Snow joke

In setting up the Awesome Eight golf challenge, founder Robin Sieger chose to play the eight courses in their most extreme conditions. This took him to the world's coldest course – North Star Golf Club, Alaska – in December. As temperatures plummeted to -26˚C (-15˚F), his golf ball shattered.

The eight venues chosen to make up the challenge are all "proper" golf clubs. Sieger picked them for their extreme characteristics, geographical or otherwise. Finding the northernmost was easy – North Cape in Norway, 300 miles (483km) inside the Arctic Circle – has no close challengers. The six-hole course is set in two long fields and has a portable cabin for a clubhouse. It offers midnight golf for six months of the year, and is charming yet unsophisticated. "Golf as played in 1902," says Sieger.

The southernmost was also a simple choice. It is Ushuaia Golf Club in southern Argentina, at 55 degrees latitude and close to Cape Horn. It is in the Tierra del Fuego National Park. The course is

flanked by snow-clad mountains, and a strong cold wind blasts up from the Antarctic.

Highest and lowest were more of a problem. The record books says Tuctu, in Peru, is the highest at 14,400 feet (4,401m), but the course has fallen into disrepair and is never used. So Sieger settled on La Paz Golf Club, Bolivia, at 10,650 feet (3,246m) the self-proclaimed loftiest links in the world. It was a similar story for the lowest: after the demise of a course near the Dead Sea, which was 320 feet (98m) below sea level, Furnace Creek in Death Valley, California, took the honours. Its first tee is 214 feet (65m) below.

Sieger also wanted to include the world's hottest and coldest courses. After consulting the British

Meteorological Office he chose Alice Springs Golf Club, in the red centre of Australia and 200 miles (322km) from Uluru (Ayers Rock), as the hottest. When he played there in mid-December, Sieger's thermometer recorded a temperature of 52°C (126°F). The prize for the coldest course went to North Star Golf Club, near Fairbanks in Alaska. Sieger played the course under snow and at a temperature of -26°C (-15°F). His golf ball shattered.

Completing the octet are the hardest course, Ko'olau Golf Club in Oahu, Hawaii and the greatest, St Andrews Old Course in Scotland. Ko'olau has a slope rating of 162, compared with 152 at Augusta National, home of the Masters tournament. "If you miss the fairway on either side, you have lost the ball," says Sieger. "It is very long too; it took us five hours and 20 minutes to play."

Sieger chose St Andrews as the greatest course, because of its historical significance as the Home of Golf. "You can't ignore it," he argues. "You are walking in the footsteps of every great golfer who's ever lived, with the exception of Ben Hogan."

Sieger decided he would be the first to complete the challenge, and set off with colleague Neil Laughton, an adventurer who has scaled the Seven Summits and is the first person to have circumnavigated the UK on a jet-ski. They decided to time their attempt so that they played the hottest course at the hottest time of year, and the coldest course at the chilliest. They made it with a day to

spare, and the record stands at 364 days for all eight courses. "I reckon it would be possible to do it in 31 days though," Sieger says.

Sieger and Laughton used the trip to raise money for the Pattaya Children's Orphanage Trust in Thailand, where Sieger has sponsored a child since 1991. Sieger respectfully requests that any charity money raised by others taking on the Awesome Eight should also go to the orphanage.

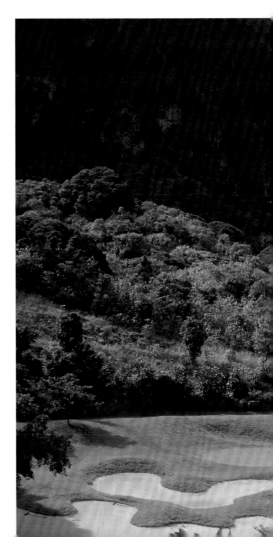

▶ Humble in the jungle

The Awesome Eight challenge identifies Ko'olau Golf Club, Hawaii, as the world's hardest course. Its design sees 14 drives over a ravine, 109 bunkers and fairways flanked by dense jungle. Gales of up to 40mph (64kph) buffet you while high rainfall means limited run on the fairways. The course has brought even the finest golfers to their knees – Costa Rican star Chi Chi Rodriguez shot 88 on his debut.

If you want to make an attempt, you must contact the Awesome Eight website (see the gazetteer, page 157) and indicate the date you plan to start. You must take a photograph of yourself at each course as verification, and get a scorecard signed by your partner. Sieger knows it is possible to fake it, but believes there's not much point. "This is an opportunity to push yourself to do something outside your comfort zone. Along the way you will meet people who will change the way you will see the world, and you will change the way you see yourself. You will discover that underneath the surface, people who love the game of golf love it for the same reasons. It is a universal brotherhood. And in ten years' time, all members of the Awesome Eight Society will meet up somewhere extreme for a game of golf and to swap some stories."

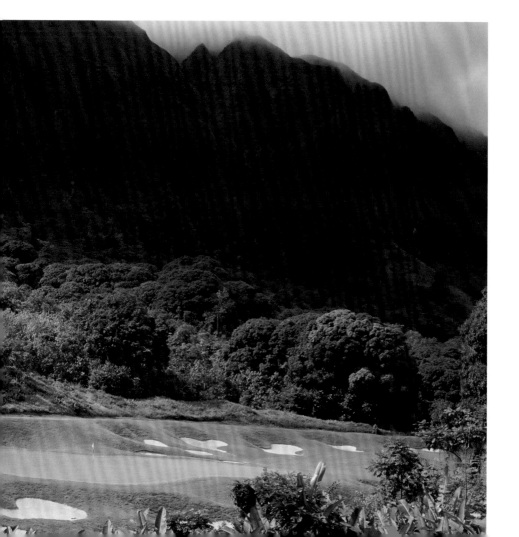

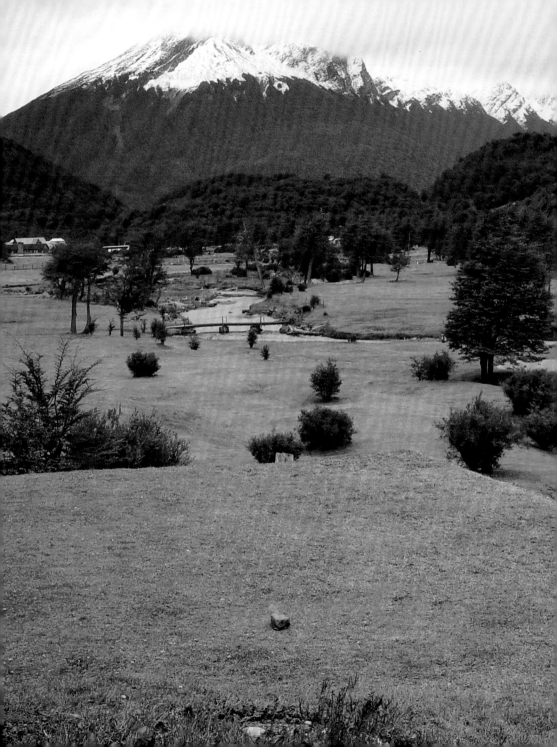

Ushuaia Golf Club

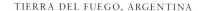

THE WORLD'S MOST SOUTHERLY GOLF COURSE

WHEN THE NATURALIST Charles Darwin first saw the land on which the world's southernmost course now sits, he wrote: "A single glance at the landscape was sufficient to show me how widely different it was from anything I had ever beheld." What he saw was a fabulously muscular panorama of forests, glaciers, beaches and mountains – fitting grandeur for a place that has come to be known as the "End of the World". It is not a bad spot for a spectacular golf course, either.

Ushuaia Golf Club lies at the southern tip of South America, at latitude 55 degrees south. It is in the Argentine province of Tierra del Fuego ("land of fire"), just a sperm whale's spout from Cape Horn. Tierra del Fuego got its name from the many beach fires built by aborigines there, which were first observed by Ferdinand Magellan in 1520, and then later by Darwin.

The course is 4 miles (6km) south of Ushuaia, the world's southernmost city, next to the Tierra del Fuego National Park.

◀ **Southern discomfort**
The snow-capped peaks of the Isla Navarino mountains form a thrilling backdrop to the nine-hole course at Ushuaia, the world's most southerly course. Golfers must plot their way around the fast-flowing Rio Pipo, which comes into play on five holes. They must also wrap up to survive the icy Antarctic blasts that drive north from Cape Horn.

"Your first view of the course is a spectacular one," says Neil Laughton, who played the course during the Awesome Eight Golf Challenge. "The only access road is a rough track, 500 feet (152m) up, that runs round the mountain that dominates the course's backdrop. You look down on the whole layout."

At the end of this dusty road is the small clubhouse, little more than a hut, which looks a bit like a ski lodge. Poky it may be, but you will find a friendly face in there ready to serve you coffee, soda or beer. If feeling adventurous, you can order fried penguin and a mug of yerba mate, a herbal tea packed with vitamins and nutrients. Yerba mate is reputed to improve athletic performance,

reduce blood pressure and boost your libido.

The course is a challenging, rough and ready nine-holer. Its dominant feature is a river, the Rio Pipo, a fiercely flowing gusher fed by massive snowmelt from the Andes. The river comes into play on five holes, and at times reaches up to 18 feet (5m) across. Should you fall in, the flow may well sweep you away. The Rio Pipo makes the 8th the course's best hole, where it frames the green at the end of a long and narrow par-5.

Laughton says a round here is far removed from a cosseted, country-club style experience. "It's not in great condition compared with Europe and America," he advises, "but for golfers like me who are prepared to rough it a bit, it's great. I found the scenery, location and general layout of the course breathtaking.

"The acreage for the course is dictated by the natural terrain; clearly they have designed the course to fit the land, rather than altered the land to suit the course. There are holes that cut across sunken embankments, others where you must hit over trees and bushes to get to the fairways – or through large pines to get to the green, like on the short 3rd. There are lots of corners to cut. You always have to play at your best to survive."

The Ushuaia golfer is also blessed with a wonderful variety of scenic backdrops. The south Atlantic is 5 miles (8km) to the east; immediately to the north are snow-capped mountains; and 20 miles (32km) to the west are the Andes, which dominate Ushuaia itself. The city is the main gateway to the Antarctic, just 730 miles (1,175km) to the south.

When Darwin went ashore he gave the natives red

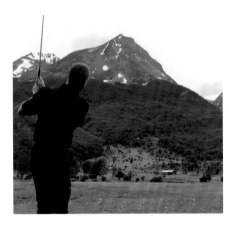

▲ Latitude attitude
Ushuaia Golf Club members are very proud of their club's status as the world's southernmost course. They give visitors a very warm welcome, and although the clubhouse is small there is plenty to eat and drink including fried penguin. They will also point out to you which of the many mountain peaks will help you find the best line off the tee.

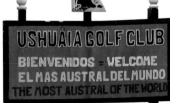

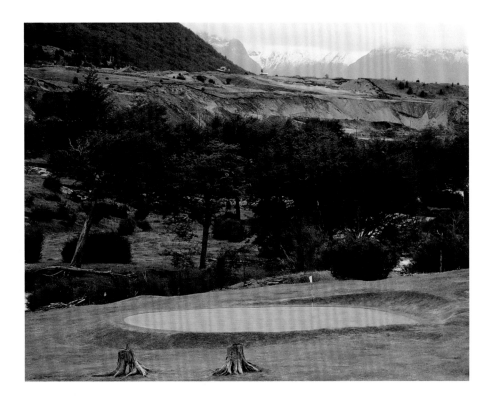

▲ Harsh but fair

Ushuaia's layout is not long but does demand accuracy, particularly around the greens which are small and difficult to hold. The course blends in to the natural landscape, and there are plans to build another nine holes in the hillside.

scarves as presents, and found to his amazement that they wore little more, even in the extreme cold and constant freezing gales. The weather is no different today. The prevailing winds come from the west and from the Antarctic, but the golfers of Ushuaia are not so hardy as those natives. Thick jumpers, lots of layers and windstoppers are the order of the day.

The course is open for seven months of the year (from October to May). For much of this period, there is enough light to play right through from 6am to 11pm. As with Norway's North Cape Golf Club, the world's most northerly course, the members are delighted with their club's unique location. The sign outside the clubhouse reads: "The most austral club in the world". During your round you are likely to see fantastic birdlife, imported Canadian beavers and red foxes. You will not see a shed for the greenkeeper's equipment, however; he keeps all his mowers and gear on the back of a red pick-up truck.

La Paz Golf Club

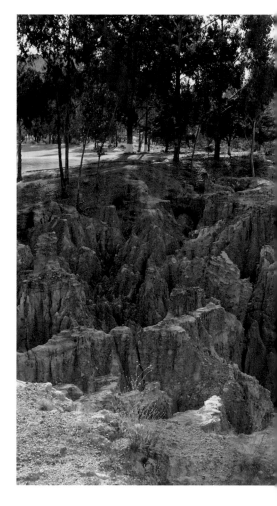

GOLFING IN THE CLOUDS

LA PAZ IS THE LOFTIEST golf course in the world. Its high point is 10,650 feet (3,246m) above sea level, so your round of golf here will take place 2 miles (3.2km) above the ocean. The air at this altitude is so thin that you can confidently expect to add 30 yards (27m) to the average 5-iron shot – instead of 170 yards (155m), it will soar more than 200 yards (183m). You will never hear a member of the La Paz Golf Club sigh: "I wish I could hit the ball like Tiger Woods" because most of them already do.

It gets even better for golfers. "The ball seems to fly straighter as well as further," says course supervisor Pablo Ignacio Fierro. "You can see it even when you kick a football. It does not bend as much. Altitude is the golfer's friend."

At least, that is, so long as you can still breathe. For the non-acclimatized, oxygen is hard to come by here and breathlessness is a common problem. The phrase "dizzy heights" becomes particularly apposite as you lumber up the hills of the course. The highland peoples of Bolivia and Peru have even coined their own word to express this feeling of breathlessness: *soroghe*.

The best advice for visiting golfers is to spend a few days at altitude before playing, and to drink plenty of water during your round. Mercifully, the club has an army of 150 caddies ready to shoulder your bag and help you on your way.

Despite its sky-scraping position, La Paz Golf Club is actually 1,150 feet (351m) below the Bolivian capital itself, and about a 20-minute drive from the city centre. At no stage, however, can you

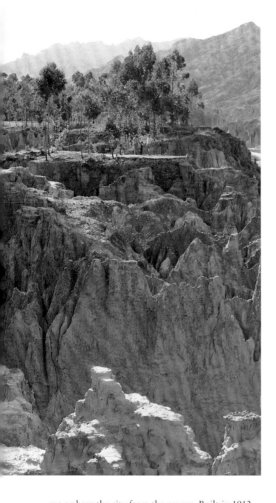

◀ Walking on the moon
La Paz Golf Club's signature moonscape has formed as a result of the local soft sandstone being slowly chiselled by thousands of years of wind and rain, adding a surreal dimension to playing the course. There are plenty of balls to be seen in the deep canyons, but no easy way of getting to them.

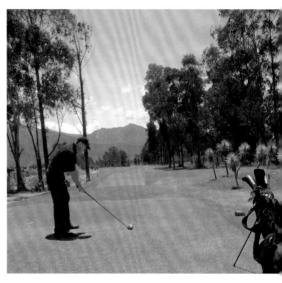

▲ No one would Bolivia

Average players can belt the ball over 300 yards (274m) at La Paz, although as Awesome Eight men Neil Laughton and Robin Sieger found, it can be hard to find someone who will credit your long-hitting claims. La Paz compensates for the extra yardage awarded by its thin air by making its holes long and tight. Trees and doglegs force you to keep your driver in the bag for most of the round.

see or hear the city from the course. Built in 1912, it is a plush country club with tennis courts and swimming pools. It is extremely welcoming, and visitors will find its holes in perfect condition – largely thanks to the low labour costs and high staffing levels. The green fee works out at roughly half the average Bolivian weekly wage.

The course is startlingly green, with plenty of trees to keep you occupied. It has also been cunningly designed to nullify the advantage of that high-altitude bionic ball flight. Doglegs and strategically sited greens place a premium on

> "I think the 12th is the most exciting hole in the world. You must cross two bridges over the moonscape just to make it to the tee. Once there, you should take a few moments to drink in the scene."

PABLO IGNACIO FIERRO

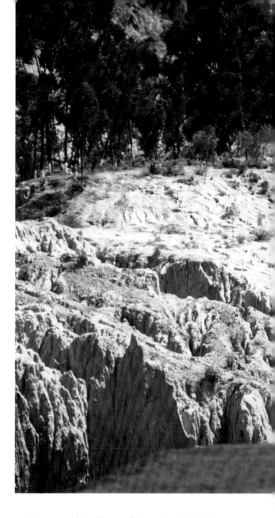

accuracy, not power. And although a couple of the par-5s measure 580 yards (530m), even the longest hitters have no chance of getting up in two.

But the most striking feature comes at the 12th hole. Suddenly, the vivid green gives way to an extraordinary lunar landscape. The soft sandstone that surrounds the city of La Paz has been patiently sculpted into crazy canyons and proud pinnacles by millennia of driving rain and howling winds. The result is a heavily pitted lunar terrain, with canyons that plumb depths of 60 feet (18m). The course is not just the closest to the moon on earth; it is also the one that most resembles it.

"I think the 12th is the most exciting hole in the world," says Fierro. "You must cross two bridges over the moonscape just to make it to the tee. Once there, you should take a few moments to drink in the scene. Behind you is an immense canyon, with snow-flecked mountains beyond it. Turn around and in front of you are 180 yards (165m) of creamy-brown crevices. Beyond that is the lush emerald fairway. And then above you, if you are lucky, are swooping condors, waiting to see if you can fly the ball all the way to the green."

Many record books award the title of "World's Highest Golf Club" to nine-hole Tuctu, in Peru, at an altitude of 14,440 feet (4,401m); but sadly this club is now grassed over and in no state for play. Members of La Paz are proud to claim the distinction in its stead: *El campo de golf mas alto del mundo*, proclaim the signs.

It is only fitting that the city of La Paz should have such a spectacular course. At 12,400 feet

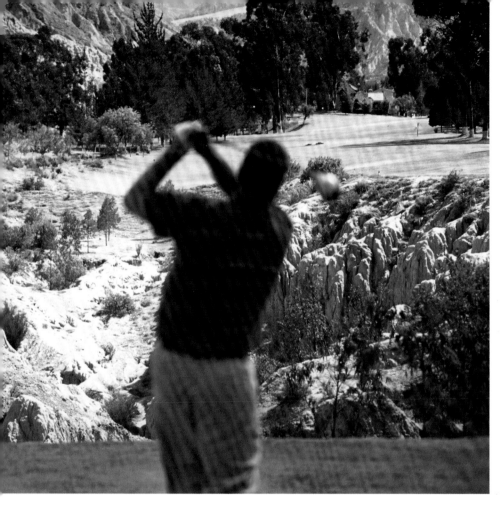

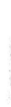

(3,780m) it is the world's highest capital, and its roads and houses are crammed into a cosmic cleft in the surrounding *altiplano* that spans 2.5 miles (4km) from rim to rim. Yet despite this serene location, the city has major traffic congestion problems and has become a hotbed for environmental protestors. La Paz means "peace" – and while there may be precious little of that in the city, you'll certainly find it on the 12th tee.

▲ **Wheeze in the trees**

La Paz is 10,650 feet (3,246m) above sea level and a round here takes place 2 miles (3.2km) above the sea level. Although the course is a reasonably easy walk, the low oxygen levels in the air means locals advise coming a few days early to acclimatize, and drinking plenty of water during the round.

▶ **Reach for the sky** (OVERLEAF)

To reach the 12th tee at La Paz, the world's highest course, you must cross two bridges over an astonishing lunar landscape. This amazing hole is the zenith of a layout that sits more than 2 miles (3.2km) above the sea.

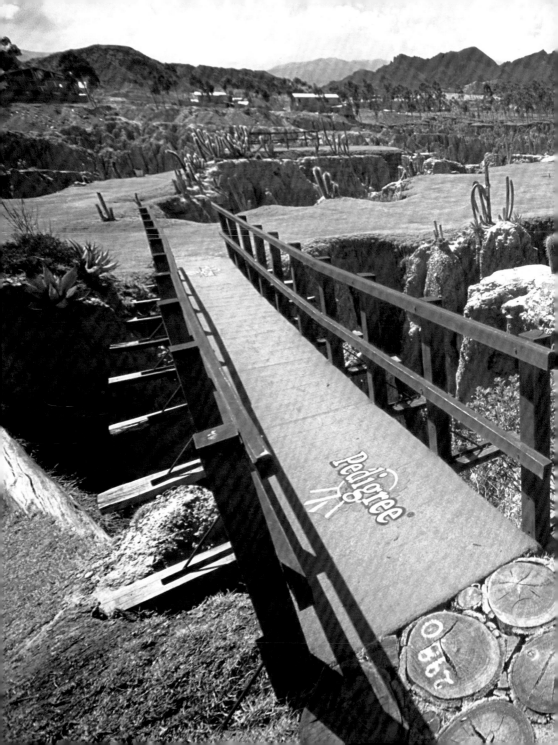

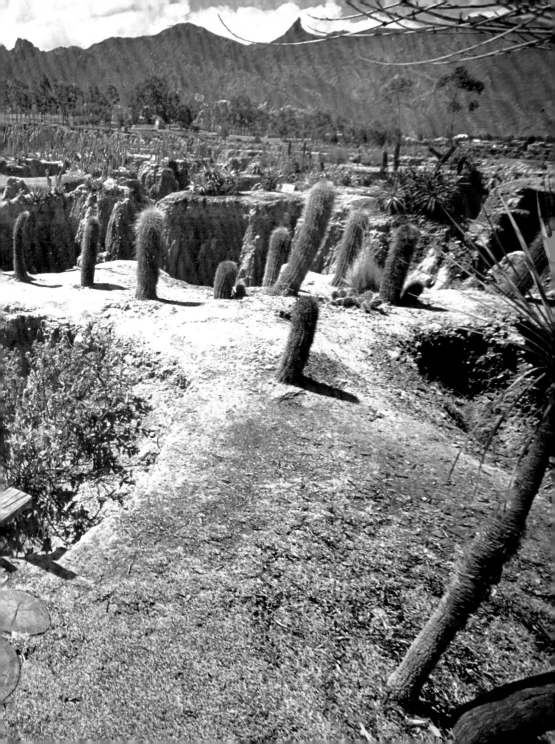

Furnace Creek Resort

THE WORLD'S LOWEST GOLF COURSE

RIGHT IN THE HEART of Death Valley, California, lies the world's lowest course. A big sign by the 1st tee informs you that you're 214 feet (65m) below sea level, just 68 feet (21m) higher than nearby Badwater, the lowest point in the whole of the Americas. Its name is the Furnace Creek Resort, and it sits in an austere no-man's land called the Mojave desert, 120 miles (193km) west of Las Vegas and 300 miles (483km) east of Los Angeles.

Short hitters will be sorry to hear that, even at 214 feet (65m) below sea level, the air thickens sufficiently to rob your ball of a few yards.

"Certainly the low altitude has an effect," agrees head professional Kip Freeman. "If you hit a 5-iron 170 yards (155m) in regular conditions, you will find it travels 150-155 yards (137-142m) here. But the course allows for that: it is only 6,200 yards (5,669m) off the back tees."

The chunkier air does not seem to trouble the more regular visitors to the course, however.

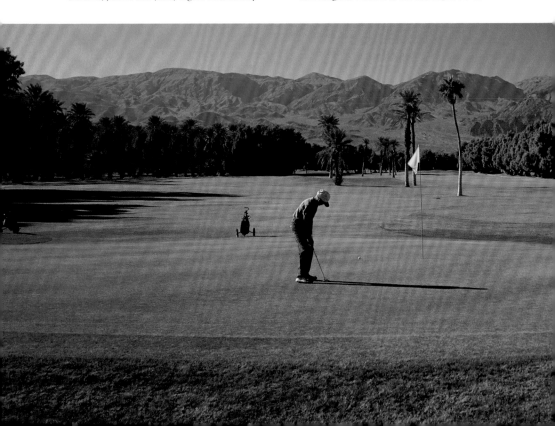

The members of one society, who for some reason have titled themselves "The Bummers", pitch up every week from the nearby town of Parhrump. "We don't mind that it's hot and the ball doesn't travel as far," says head Bummer Terry Moriarty. "You just adapt to it. There's no hardship in taking an extra club. We carry on playing right through the summer."

Furnace Creek is a regular resort course – flattish, not too tight and punctuated by occasional tamarisk and date palm trees. Its holes appear ludicrously green against the barren desert and the Panamint mountains that surround it. And despite the arid location – Death Valley gets an average 1.6 inches (4.1cm) of rainfall a year – water hazards come into play on six holes.

The extreme heat means that the resort has needed to install a sophisticated irrigation system to water the holes when they need it, rather than at set intervals through the day. "The golf course gets its water from natural underground springs, which feed the creek that runs through it," explains Freeman. "In the height of summer we throw a million gallons (4.5 million litres) a day onto the course. On an average day the figure will be more than 200,000 gallons (900,000 litres)."

▼ **Low heat**
Golfers putt out 214 feet (65m) below sea level at Death Valley's Furnace Creek, the lowest golf course in the world. Ground temperature in the valley floor is 40 per cent higher than the air temperature, and an astonishing ground reading of 94°C (201°F) was recorded at Furnace Creek in 1972.

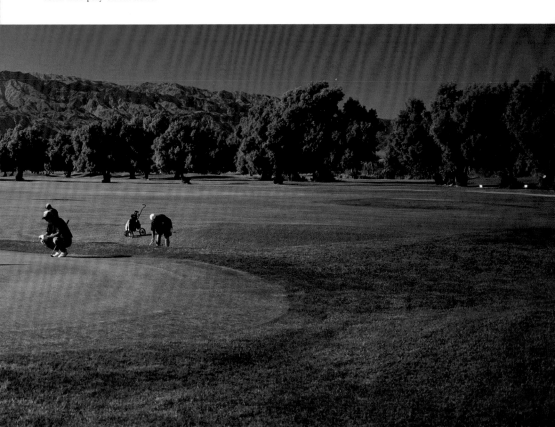

So how did a golf course come to be in such a curious location? Bizarrely, it's all to do with sodium borate (borax), which was discovered occuring naturally in Death Valley in the late nineteenth century. Back then it was prized as a magical crystal, and used to aid digestion, preserve milk and even cure epilepsy. Today borax has any number of applications, including a role in the storage of nuclear waste.

Keen to cash in, the US Pacific Coast Borax Company set up mining camps here in 1881. But Death Valley did not offer the employees much in the way of entertainment, so the company built the Furnace Creek resort, complete with golf course. Three holes opened in 1927, became nine in the 1930s and finally 18 in the 1950s.

The resort has introduced several measures to make golfing in this desolate place as comfortable as possible. A marvellous outdoor grill operates all day, and the beer is always served extra-chilled. But best of all is the clubhouse drive-thru. From a phone on the 9th tee, you can ring up, dry-throated, and croak your snack order to the people at the 19th. You then drive your buggy off the 9th green and up onto a ramp to pick up your food and drink. Then off you go to the 10th tee.

It is not unusual to play your golf here amid a chorus of coyote howls. Coyotes pad across the course regularly, and they'll generally ignore you so long as you keep a respectful distance. There have, however, been reported cases of coyotes picking up balls and dropping them again – apparently inviting players to chase them, puppy-dog style. If you do, the confounded hound will simply pick up the ball again and carry it off to a safe distance. Only when you drop another and play on will he get bored and run off – with ball in mouth.

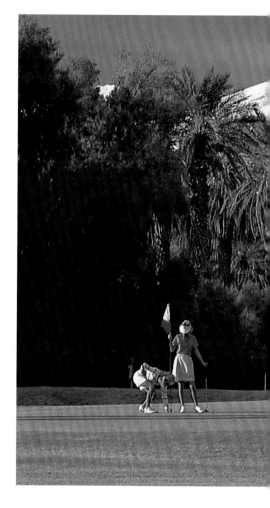

Coyotes or not, the stillness and remoteness of Furnace Creek make playing here a singular experience. "I think the feeling you get is one of peace," says Freeman. "There's no traffic, no hustle and bustle, and we certainly won't make you dash around the course – unlike the coyotes."

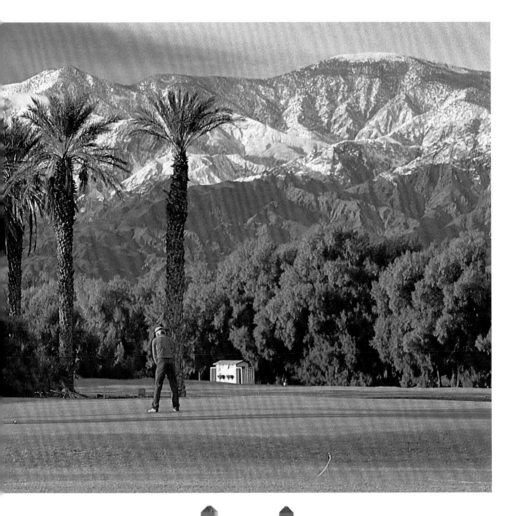

▲ How green is my valley?

The fairways of Furnace Creek need 200,000 gallons (900,000 litres) of water a day, yet Death Valley averages 1.6 inches (4.1cm) of rain a year. The course water sprinklers are supplied by huge underground aquifers.

WELCOME TO
FURNACE CREEK G.C.
WORLDS LOWEST GOLF COURSE
214 FEET
BELOW
SEA
LEVEL

▶ Twilight zone (OVERLEAF)

Furnace Creek is aptly named – intense day-time heat makes golfing in the evening far more pleasurable, although you will still have to contend with short-hitting caused by the thick air, while keeping an eye out for hunting coyotes that will make off with your ball.

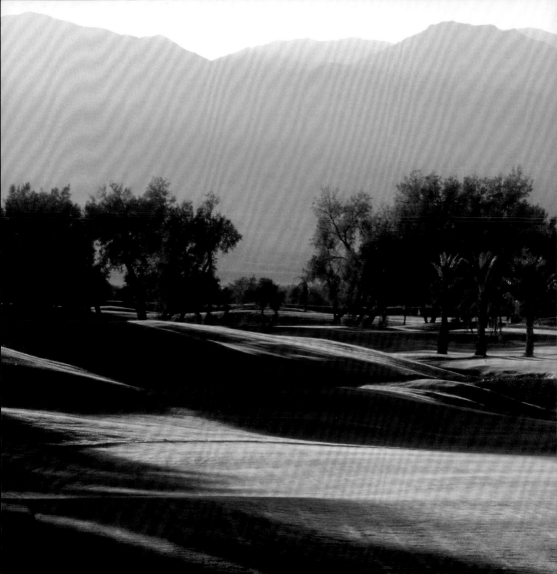

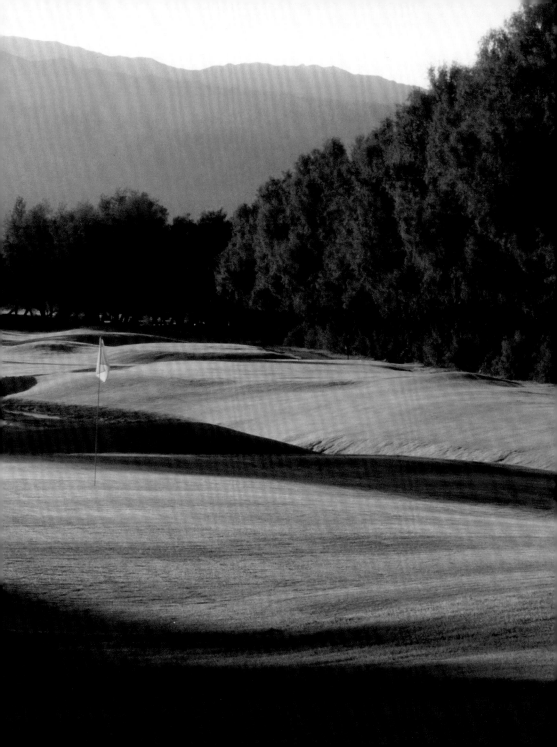

Alice Springs Golf Club

THE HOTTEST
GOLF COURSE ON EARTH

THERE ARE WATER CANISTERS on every third tee at Alice Springs Golf Club. The water is primarily for drinking, but when Robin Sieger and Neil Laughton of the Awesome Eight Golf Challenge played here, they dunked towels into them and wrapped the sopping wet material around their heads. "The towels were bone dry seven minutes later," reveals Sieger. "We timed it."

Alice Springs Golf Club can justifiably claim to be the hottest golf course on earth. It swelters on the outskirts of Alice Springs town, 200 miles

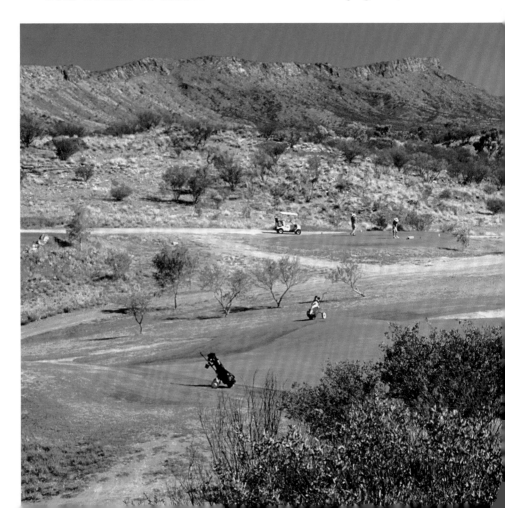

(322km) from Uluru (Ayers Rock) and deep in Australia's heartland. Sieger recalls that when he began his round the temperature was 44°C (111°F), but quickly rose to 52°C (126°F). It gets so hot that the local highways department constantly monitors the roads to see which ones are melting.

▼ **Fan-assisted oven**

As if temperatures rising to 50°C (122°F) are not enough to deal with, strong, hot winds whistle across the fairways of the world's hottest course. Even though water is in plentiful supply, playing through the heat of the day is not advised.

As well as being the hottest golf club in the world, Alice Springs may well be the friendliest. As soon as you set foot in the clubhouse, someone will be shaking your right hand and putting a beer in your left. You will receive plenty of sage advice about the risks of heat stroke on the hottest days, but the members won't stop you going out to play. You can confidently expect to have both the course to yourself and your sanity called into question.

Until 1992 this course was no more than a scrubby desert track with oil-based greens, built on

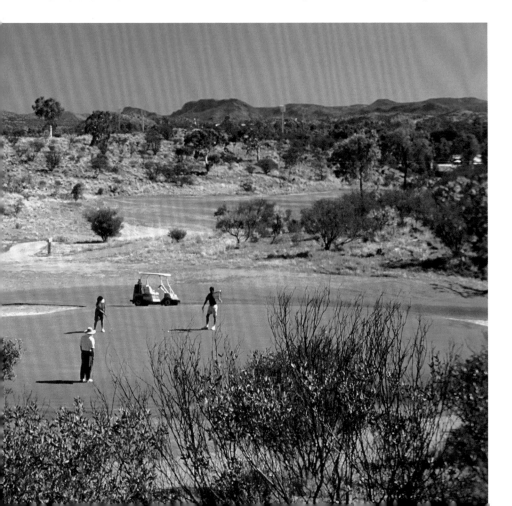

the searing magenta earth that characterises this part of the world. But the club wanted grass, and toiled to install an irrigation system. A lush green course grew out of the rubble, and today's 18-holer is a pleasure to play – so long as you don't start at midday in December, like Sieger did.

The layout is flattish, its main hazard the parched scrub that flanks the entire course. There are also plenty of bunkers which bounce heat and light straight back at you, and one water hazard on the 18th.

During the course of your round, however, you are likely to come across a less familiar hazard. Giant goanna lizards roam the course, some of them up to 3 feet (0.9m) long, their huge tails

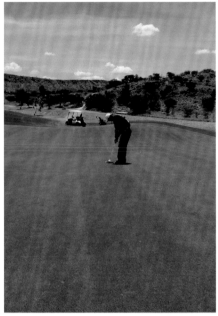

▼▶ **Rough with the smooth**
The course at Alice Springs had sand greens up until 1985 when an ambitious plan to irrigate the course was put into action. Water from the Todd River, 1 mile (1.6km) to the west, quickly turned the course from brown to green.

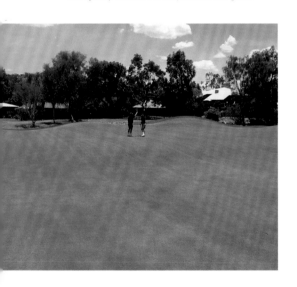

swishing back and forth as if mimicking the smoothest putting stroke. They will ignore you, and it is best not to panic them. When frightened, however, their instincts tell them to run up a tree. The trouble is that they have very poor eyesight, and cannot distinguish between a golfer and the native acacia peuce.

If you get lucky, you may also see a camel or two. Camels were introduced to Australia in 1840, after pioneers pushing eastwards from the coast discovered horses and donkeys were not hardy enough to cope with the extreme heat and aridity. Camels do graze wild here, but many others are put to work by the townsfolk of Alice Springs. They are also a tourist draw, and a camel race, the Camel Cup, is held every July.

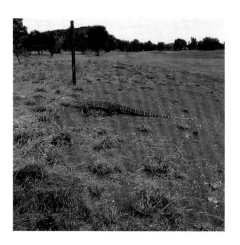

▲ **Lizard kings**

Giant goannas roam the course at Alice Springs Golf Club, Australia – the world's hottest course. The Awesome Eight's Robin Sieger played here in the height of summer and his temperature gauge rose to 52°C (126°F). The goannas have poor eyesight and can mistake humans for trees; they have been known to run up a golfer's leg when cornered.

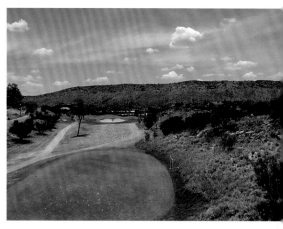

▲▼ **Spikey problem**

The holes at Alice Springs are surrounded by spinifex (also called porcupine grass) which has pointed leaves and spiny seed heads. Usually planted to keep moving sand at bay, it is uncompromising stuff which lets a clubhead through only grudgingly. You are best off keeping the ball in play than taking on long, narrow shots.

Apart from the heat, there is a profound sense of remoteness. Alice Springs may not quite be the dusty outback hamlet portrayed in *A Town Like Alice*: its population has reached 27,000. Nevertheless, it is more than 900 miles (1,450km) from the nearest major city, Adelaide.

One of the features of playing golf here is the stunning colour changes you will witness in the nearby Macdonnell foothills. These low mountains frame the course, and the spectacle of their shifting hues is referred to in Nevil Shute's novel *A Town Like Alice*. Shute's hero, Joe Harmon, describes "great red ranges against the blue sky. And in the evenings they go purple and all sorts of colours. And silvery-white in the dry. And after the wet, they're green all over."

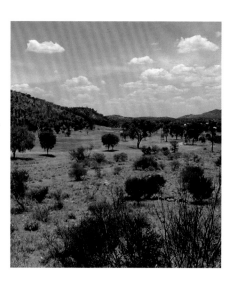

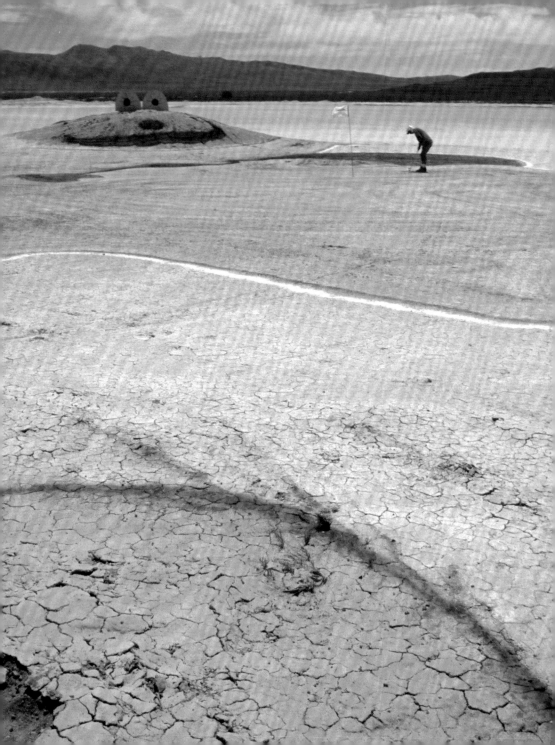

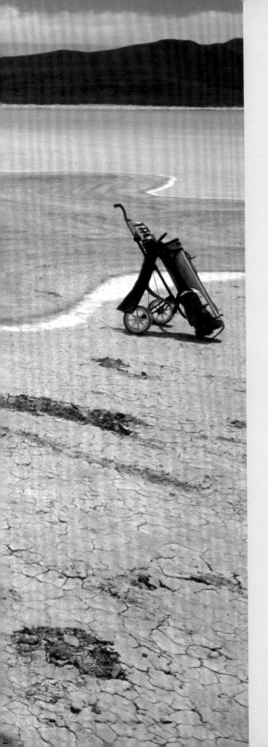

2

In the Rough

Players at Lucifer's Anvil Golf Course in the middle of Nevada's Black Rock Desert experience one of America's bleakest landscapes. If you want to play golf on extreme terrain, but don't fancy this exceptionally arid landscape, you have no shortage of options. How about golfing on glaciers, expansive clay flats, through bubbling mud pools or up and down mountains?

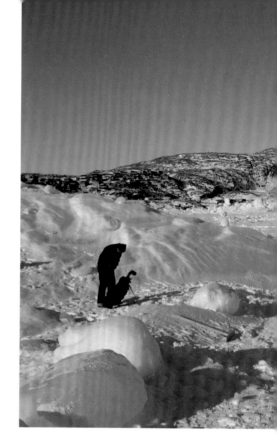

The World Ice Golf Championship

ⵏ

GOLFING ON GLACIERS

GREENLAND IN MARCH is not the most hospitable place. The average temperature is -14°C (6.8°F), but the mercury frequently plummets to -25°C (-13°F). Ice freezes 30 feet (9.1m) thick. Brilliant sunshine flashes off the pristine white land surface, making snow-blindness a serious danger. Sudden Arctic gales howl across the tundra, whipping up the powdery snow and adding a wind chill that can take the air against your skin to a frostbiting -50°C (-58°F). Yet it was in March that the tiny Inuit village of Uummannaq, 367 miles (590km) north of the Arctic Circle, hosted the Drambuie World Ice Golf Championship for

> "If you love golf, this tournament beats everything you've done in your golf career. It's an adventure I will never forget."
>
> ⵏ
>
> MICHAEL DOMBERGER

five years, from its inauguration in 1999 until 2003. In 2004 the event is being hosted for the first time by Svalbad in Norway.

One of 11 ice golf tournaments worldwide, the event's success proves once again that golfers revel in the chance to test their skills in the harshest possible conditions: each year there are 36 places up for grabs, and the organisers at Uummannaq had no problem filling them. Michael Domberger, from Germany, sums up the thrill of playing in the championship: "It was one of the most spectacular trips of my life, filled with unexpected sights and events. If you love golf, this tournament beats

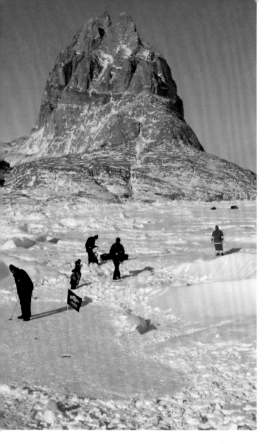

◀ Slippery putt

At the Drambuie World Ice Golf Championship the greens – more accurately whites – are formed from metre-thick pack ice. This nine-hole course is constructed afresh every year as the Uummannaq fjord freezes. Competitors are allowed to sweep the snow off their line with a broom.

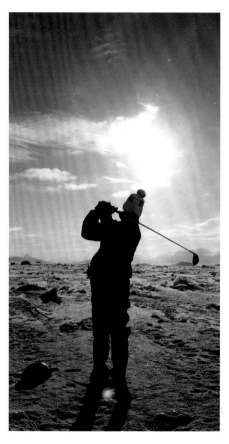

everything you've done in your golf career. It's an adventure I will never forget."

When competitors arrive at Uummannaq, they are taken to a hotel owned by Arne Neimann, the man who came up with the world ice golf concept, where they stay for the duration of the event. There is no danger of them oversleeping and missing their tee time: they are woken at dawn every morning by the haunting sound of howling huskies.

The Uummannaq championship is contested over two days and four strokeplay rounds, on an astonishing nine-hole course. The holes are laid out on icebergs that have broken off from a nearby

▲ Hitting into the sun

In temperatures that can plummet to -50˚C (-58˚F), the sun does help to provide a little much-needed warmth. It does not make the ice golfer's task any easier, however, with snow blindness being a serious problem.

► Ice tee anyone?

*Players are allowed to use a rubber tee when on the fairway.
It is also strongly advised that golfers play with a red ball.
While not compulsory, competitors who have rigidly stuck
to a traditional white ball have lived to regret it.*

▼ Getting the drift

*Golfers are allowed to tee their ball up as long as it comes
to rest between 'fairways', marked out by flags. If you slice
or hook, your punishment is usually an improbable thrash
at a snow drift. Competitors report a dreamlike sense of
detachment as they disappear behind drifts and icebergs to
play recovery shots.*

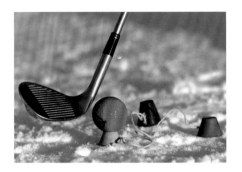

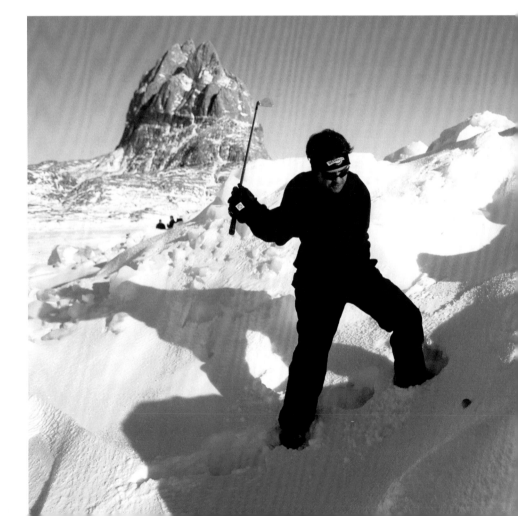

glacier and drifted into the fjord, only to be trapped as the sea freezes. This makes for a dynamic landscape, and returning players have often been dismayed to discover that the holes they mastered the previous year have been replaced by glistening walls of ice.

The course is short – usually a little under 3,000 yards (2,743m) – to compensate for golf swings restricted by seven layers of thermal clothing and a *de rigueur* sealskin jacket. But it

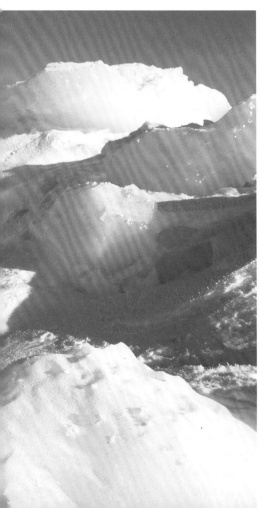

also helps the players to cope with golf balls that fly like shuttlecocks as they freeze in mid-air.

The Uummannaq tournament committee likes to maintain a par of 35 or 36, and ideally looks to route five par-4s, two par-3s and two par-5s through the pillars of ice. Fairways are marked out by flags, and when on the fairway a competitor is allowed to place the ball on a rubber tee. Greens are called "whites". They are fashioned from brushed pack ice 3 feet (0.9m) thick, covered with a dusting of snow. A broom is available to sweep your line, which your ball will hold very well, and the cup is twice the size of a regular hole.

Players must also choose their weapons carefully – no-one uses graphite shafts because they shatter in the cold. Most golfers use a red ball (there is nothing to stop traditionalists using a white ball, but nobody doing so has ever fared very well in the tournament). Everyone wears sunglasses.

"The players must be prepared for the fact that the foundation of the course is variable and can be very different from hole to hole," says project manager Preben Kaspersen. "There can be a lot more snow on one side of an iceberg than the other. Also, the ice is very different from that on, say, a European ice rink. On top of the hard ice there's a layer of frozen powder, 1 inch (2.5cm) thick which makes the surface rough and uneven."

Scotsman Jonathan Brown found out about the variable ground conditions the hard way. "I was about to play a shot when one of my legs suddenly disappeared through a seal's breathing hole in the ice," he shivers. "The experience must have done me some good, because after finishing last the previous year I moved up to 14th place!"

The unorthodox landscape has led the tournament committee to pass three local rules.

▶ The iceman cometh

Competitors at the World Ice Golf Championship must prepare themselves for an icy experience, and consider packing a balaclava before they make the trip.

First, when your ball lies on the white, you can move it a club's length to either side, but no nearer the hole; second, you are allowed to smooth the line of your putt with the scraper provided; and finally, if you lose a ball, you are allowed to drop another near where you deem the original ball to have been lost, under a one-stroke penalty.

The officials also sought guidance from the game's governing body, the Royal & Ancient, on what to do about polar bears, whose visits to Uummannaq are rare but not unheard of. The R&A adjudged that "in the event of a polar bear

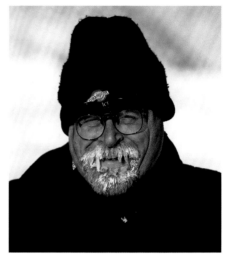

wandering onto the ice golf course, the same safety procedure should be followed as for rattlesnakes and ants elsewhere in the world." In other words, you can have a free drop out of harm's way.

Perhaps we should not be so amazed by the success of this and other ice golf extravaganzas. The Dutch game of *kolven*, a forerunner of golf, was played on frozen canals in the seventeenth century. A famous painting by Dutch artist Aert van der Neer depicts people trying to get a small ball into a hole in the ice. The World Ice Golf Championship may appear futuristic, but it is merely revisiting the game's roots.

Former entrants say the experience is surreal. "At times I had to play a shot from behind an iceberg,

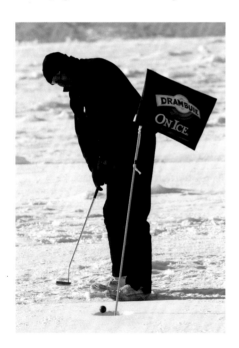

◀ The iceman putteth

Finding the cup is not made easier by the required garb. In blinding sun and freezing temperatures, golfers don gloves, sunglasses and boots, sporting several thinner layers rather than one thick one to regulate their body temperature.

blocking my view of my fellow competitors," reports American Sean Kelly. "It gave me the brief illusion that I was totally alone in these endless stretches of ice. I was playing golf with a feeling of solitude I doubt I will ever encounter again. There are many moments when players hear nothing but the wind and their own loud thoughts."

The event also promotes a marvellous sense of camaraderie among the contestants. For a non-team game, golf has a fantastic and undervalued spirit of comradeship, and this only grows when the going gets tough. "We all egg each other on and the team spirit is always brilliant," says 2002 champion Roger Beames.

One thing is for sure – the event's competitors from all corners of the globe sing the praises of the event and its course. Many, like American Jack O'Keefe, cite the beauty of the Arctic landscape as reason enough to make the long journey and brave the harsh elements. "Nothing can prepare you for this," he says. "It's like the final scene in the Superman movie, when Clark Kent flies back to Krypton. Despite the difficulties, you can't get frustrated. You just look around at this amazing country and you remember why you are here."

▼ **Uplifting tradition**
The reward for the winner is to be held aloft on a dog sled while being cheered by other competitors and the locals. In 2002 the Scot Roger Beames got the traditional treatment after seeing off American Jack O'Keefe by one shot. "While the extreme conditions of ice golf are beyond the norm, the game is basically the same," he says. "It requires skill, concentration, strategy and the right equipment."

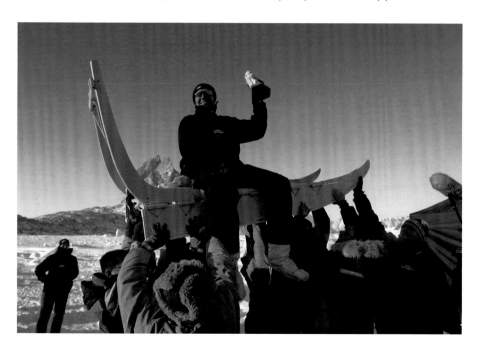

Lucifer's Anvil Golf Course

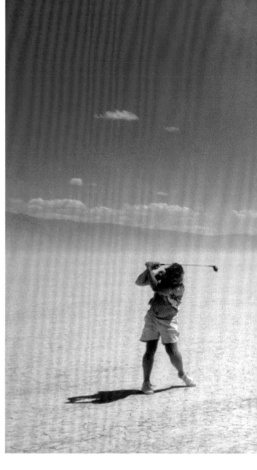

GOLFING ON CLAY IN AMERICA'S BLEAKEST LANDSCAPE

IN THE MIDDLE OF Black Rock Desert, north-west Nevada, there is a 300 square mile (777sq km) area of nothing. The nothing was a frozen lake back in the last Ice Age, but as the climate heated up and the waters departed, a vast void appeared. The alkali flats that comprise the desert floor – also known as "playa" – are so level that they are used for attempts on the world land-speed record. Man has gone faster here than anywhere else, ThrustSSC reaching 766.109mph (1232.67kph) in 1997 and breaking the speed of sound for the first time.

Man has gone pretty slowly here, too, for this is the location of Lucifer's Anvil, another of the world's most extreme golf courses. The idea of bringing golf here came from photographer Doug Keister who, in 1988, was looking for an unusual way to celebrate his 40th birthday. He succeeded and with interest, persuading some of his friends to venture into the desert for a three-hole challenge match.

"Originally we used sticks for pins and coffee tins for holes," he recalls. "Sometimes we wrapped towels or bits of underwear on the sticks for flags."

One of the first things Keister noticed about his new course was that striking a ball off the hard, baked clay was like hitting it off a road surface. The group quickly passed a local rule allowing you to tee up the ball for every shot, including putts. The ground was too hard to stick a tee peg into, but there were many cracks to take advantage of. Everyone used orange balls, correctly guessing that white ones would be impossible to spot against the pale earth.

10 MILES

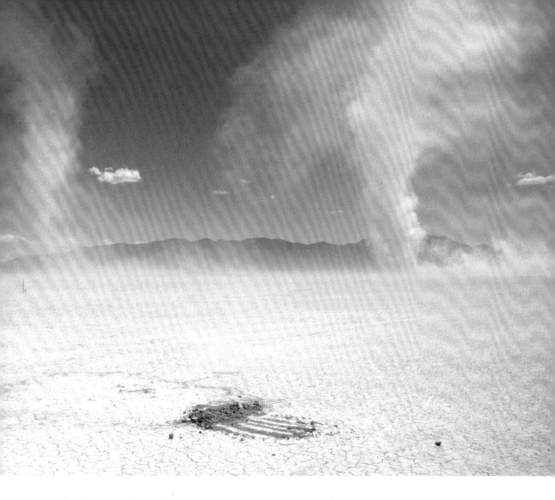

The playa is one of America's bleakest landscapes. The architect George Keller once described it thus: "The stillness of death reigns over this vast plain. Not the rustling of a leaf or the hum of an insect breaks the eternal solitude." Midday temperatures hover around the 38°C (100°F) mark, and sudden 60mph (97kph) gales blast in from nowhere to strafe the course. Yet it didn't take Keister and friends long to discover that golfing here was a lot of fun.

▲ **Drivers on the storm**

Those who've played the course at Lucifer's Anvil speak of the immense sense of liberation and freedom afforded while doing so. It is what brings players like Mark Skinner to return again and again. "It is so alien to anything you can experience in England... so incredibly liberating."

▶ **Dye hard** (OVERLEAF)

The greens of Lucifer's Anvil are made visible against the blinding, baked playa with biodegradeable spray paint. Each hole is painted to a theme. "Hell", featuring flames and demons, is the longest hole on the course.

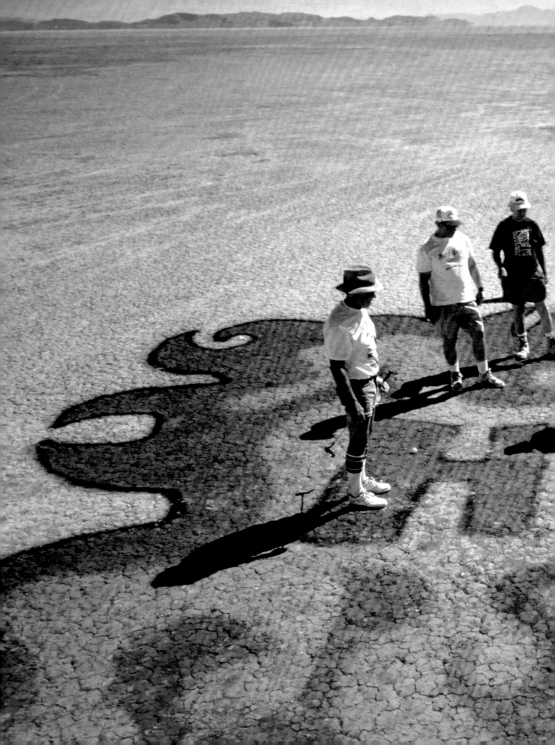

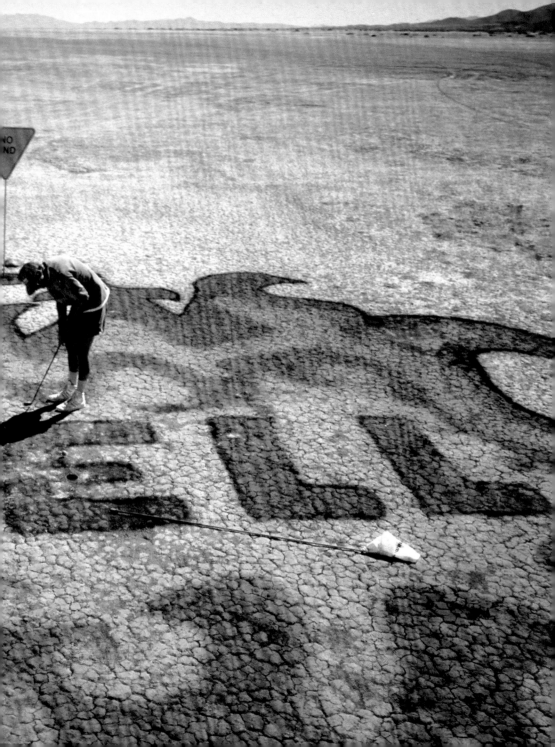

"You get this tremendous rush of freedom," he says. "This is the ultimate open space. I remember a Japanese TV crew once came out to film and they could not believe the feeling of liberation. They just walked around, filming nothingness."

Keister's birthday romp in the desert proved so successful that the group decided to turn it into an annual competition. So began the Black Rock Desert Self-Invitational, staged every June and open to all. The three-hole course quickly became nine and today measures 3,900 yards (3,566m). But the yardage is irrelevant. The hard-as-concrete surface ensures that a drive which carries 200 yards (183m) will bound on merrily for another 200 yards (183m).

The only drawback is that the second 200 yards (183m) will not always be in the same direction as the first. The surface is flat, but not *that* flat. Keister's crowd used to have a long-driving competition before the tournament proper began, but got so fed up with erratic bounces that they changed it to a nearest-the-pin event. The pin is 454 yards (415m) away, and many players have managed to get within a few paces of it.

During the competition, each group goes out with a bicycle. The format is Texas Scramble, and the player who hits the worst drive (or gets the worst bounce) has the pleasure of pedalling off to retrieve their wayward missile.

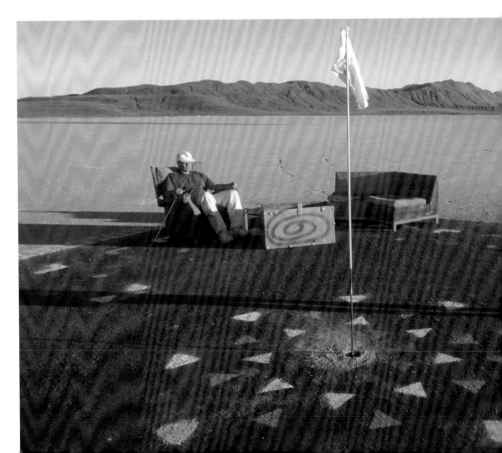

One golfer who knows that feeling is Englishman Mark Skinner, who has made the 10,000-mile (16,093km) round trip to the Black Rock Desert Self-Invitational four times. "There is something special about playing golf in such a remote location," he explains. "You drive 100 miles (161km) from the nearest big town, Reno, and another 10 miles (16km) into the desert. It is so alien to anything you can experience in England. It's incredibly liberating, and it's great not to have to worry about the little protocols of the game or what the other golfers are saying about you."

The tournament organisers have overcome difficulties with spotting the greens in the featureless landscape by colouring them with vivid biodegradable paint. The holes have developed themes. The green of the longest hole – 702 yards (642m) and known as "Hell" – features flames and demons, and the hole nearest the access track is called "Freeway", its green sprayed to resemble a road.

After 15 years of the Black Rock Desert Self-Invitational, Keister prefers to play out there than at a lush country club. "This is better than grass," he insists. "There are no pesky trees, no out-of-bounds, and the fairways are huge. You have to experience the desert to feel the significance of it. I call it the world's largest stage. Whatever you put out there becomes a fantastic thing."

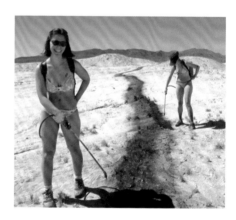

◀ **Desert art**
Every year, the designs for Lucifer's Anvil greens get a little more sophisticated and intricate. Apart from enhanced visibility, founder Doug Keister describes their purpose as "a mixture of performance art and the desire to give contestants a memory they won't forget in a hurry".

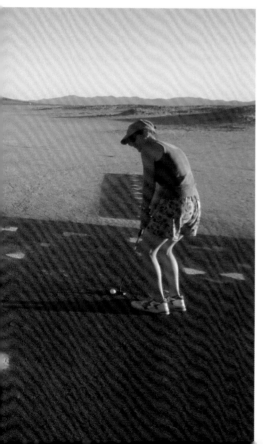

▲ **Hot work**
The Black Rock Self-Invitational is open to all; there is no dress code. As well as improving your golf, you may also be offered the chance to brush up on your spraying skills.

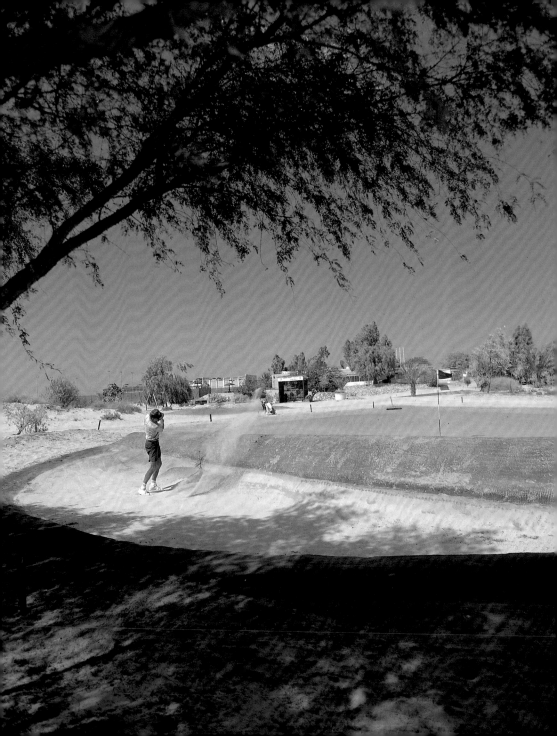

Dubai Country Club

THE BAD BUNKER PLAYER'S NIGHTMARE

THE AMERICAN COURSE architect Charles Blair Macdonald once snarled: "The object of a bunker or trap is not only to punish a physical mistake, but also to punish pride and egotism." Given that 99 per cent of bunkers achieve that goal, you might imagine that players would flee from the sandy fairways of the Dubai Country Club, a grassless course in the Arabian Desert which is basically one titanic bunker. Instead, they flock to it.

"Visitors want to play the course purely and simply for the curiosity factor," says the club's professional Kevin Hind. "It is such a different experience. People come to this part of the world with images of the sand and the sand dunes, and they find it exciting to come out and play golf among them. And they really enjoy it, especially the putting side."

There *is* grass on the golf course – but it is plastic and takes the form of a mat that you carry

◀ Grain of hope

Cheekily for a sand-based course, the Dubai Country Club course has plenty of bunkers. The sand in them is local but a finer grain, similar to the sand found in traditional western course traps.

round with you. You are allowed to hit off the mat whenever your ball lies between the green wooden stakes that define the fairways.

Playing Dubai for the first time is a memorable experience – and it was especially memorable for Hind. He shot a 64, which still stands as the course record. "The first thing that strikes you is the lack of run," he says. "Even though you know you are hitting onto sand, you somehow still expect the ball to bounce. Of course, it doesn't." In fact, the 2nd, 10th, 11th and 12th holes offer more roll than the others. Since they are exposed to the wind, their covering of sand is thinner.

"Also," Hind continues, "when playing from soft sand you become very aware of your stance and balance. If you lash at the ball with a lot of leg action, you will slide all over the place and have a nightmare. Much better to play with control."

Hind believes the all-sand course makes the long game harder, but the short game easier. The greens, or more accurately the "browns", are smoother than grass, while their surrounds demand a smaller repertoire of short-game shots.

The browns at Dubai Country Club are perhaps its biggest draw. Their surface consists of a mixture of sand and oil (no shortage of either in the United Arab Emirates), which is blended, applied and rolled by the maintenance team. Despite regular brushing, the surface is forever covered with a dusting of fine sand which means players are robbed of the much-loved excuse, "I misread the break", by the many tell-tale sand trails from previous putts. The browns stand out against the barren landscape because they are darker, and raised above the desert floor.

Compared with most greens, browns putt slower but truer. There are none of the humps and bumps

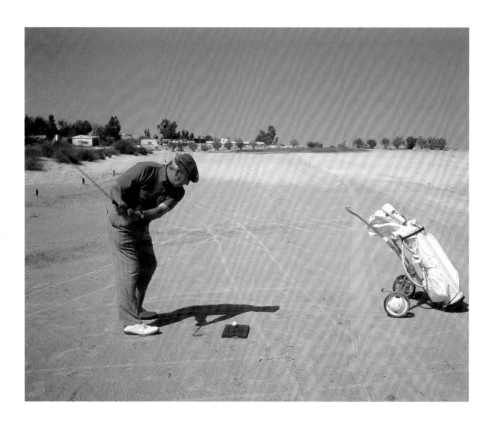

that grass provides, and no grain of course. They take chips and pitches much the same as normal greens. They will hold a well-struck iron shot, although the ball will always run forward a little on landing – even your best strike will not make the ball back-up.

Rather sadistically for a course built on sand, Dubai Country Club features plenty of grassless bunkers. They have been dug out to create conventional lips and filled with regular desert sand. This is soft and invites a buried lie, though the club has passed a local rule offering a free drop.

▲ **Sandy foundations**

If your ball winds up in a marked area you are allowed to place your ball on a piece of astroturf. Be warned though; your stance is still on sand and it is easy to slip when swinging flat out. The "browns" are a much darker colour than the surrounding sand and easy to spy.

The 6,431-yard (5,881m) course was opened in 1970, making it the first golf club in the United Arab Emirates. It has hosted the prestigious Dubai Men's Open since 1974. 10,000 gallons (45,000 litres) of water a day are required to water the course's shrubs and flowers, which sounds like

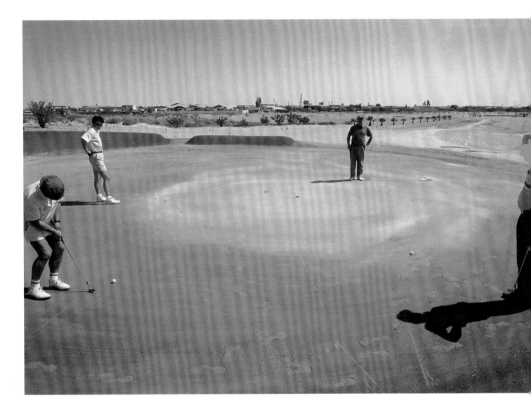

▲ Circles in the sand

The "browns" of the Dubai Country Club are made from sand and oil. They putt superbly, and canny golfers use grooves from previous putts to help them read the line. They are deceptively firm: even with a well-struck approach shot the ball will take a couple of bounces to settle down.

a lot until you discover that grassed courses in this part of the world use 1 million gallons (4.5 million litres) every 24 hours. In fact, the course's biggest enemy is rainfall: excess water can make the browns soft and mushy. But there's no need to worry too much – Dubai's average annual precipitation is just 6 inches (15.2cm), and half of that falls in February.

On a day-to-day basis the club is completely at ease with its unusual setting – one can almost imagine the members being taken aback at the sight of a green course. The only glitch occurred a few years ago, when buggies were introduced. There was a hard cart path running through the course for the golfers to use, but most mistook the buggies for 4X4s and took off into the desert in search of their balls. Staff spent the best part of a week hauling stranded caddie-cars out of the sand.

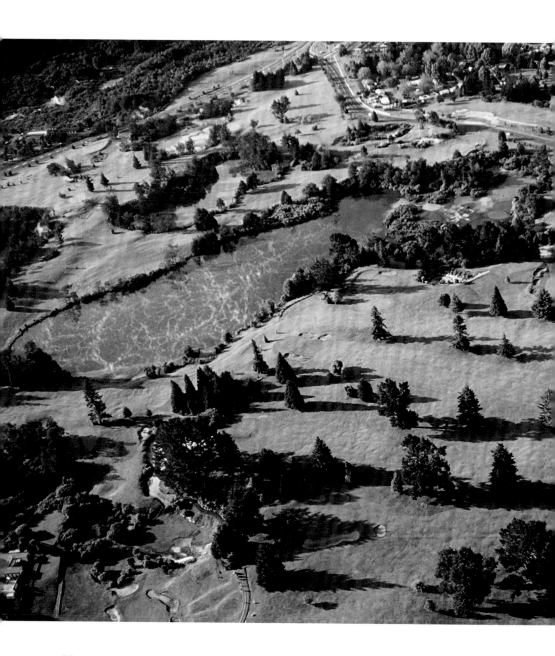

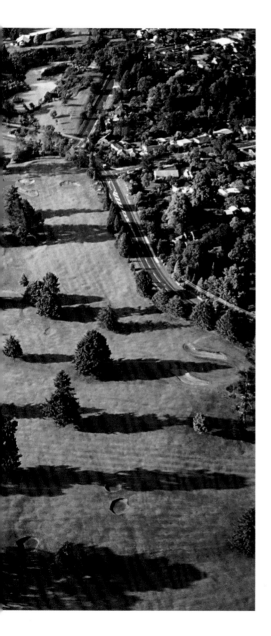

Rotorua Golf Club

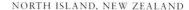

THERMAL GOLF

THE 18-HOLE GOLF COURSE at Rotorua is named Arikikapakapa. This Maori word means "the sound of plopping mud" – apt, because the course is built in the heart of a pulsating thermal zone.

A third of the course is covered by thermal lakes, bubbling mud pools, sulphur pits and steaming vents. These features have been been put to excellent use as the main tactical hazards, especially on the par-3s. On the 9th, perhaps the signature hole, you must avoid several bubbling mud pools with your tee shot. There is another mud pool to the left of the green, while to the right is a reeking yellow sulphur pit that seems to reach out and claim your ball. It is possible to play out of this pit, but you'd better hold your breath. It is also best not to use your sand wedge: the bottom of the pit is hard and compacted, and the rounded sole of the club will bounce straight off the surface. This hole has the distinction of being depicted on a Kiwi postage stamp.

◀ Hubble, bubble, toil and trouble
Thermal features dominate the Arikikapakapa course at Rotorua. Golfers playing the course, built on quick-draining pumice, must overcome bubbling mud-pools, steamy fissures and egg-stinking sulphurous pits during their round.

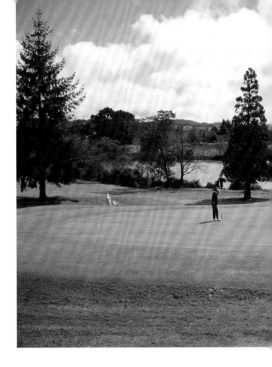

As well as the Arikikapakapa 18-holer, Rotorua has a nine-hole course, known as the "Thermal", which offers just as great a challenge. Both courses will have you wishing you had a better sense of vision but a poorer sense of smell. Golfers are greeted by the sensational sight of steam billowing from the many ground fissures sprinkled among the holes. This increases as the weather becomes colder. Holes 14, 15 and 16 on Arikikapakapa – Rotorua's Amen Corner – are played across or alongside a lake, and on a chilly winter's morning the sight of steam rising from the water is truly astonishing, not to mention a little creepy.

▼ Stamp of approval

The beauty of Rotorua's par-3 9th hole has been recognized with its appearances on a New Zealand postage stamp. Trouble lurks everywhere, but four sets of tees give the golfer an easier option.

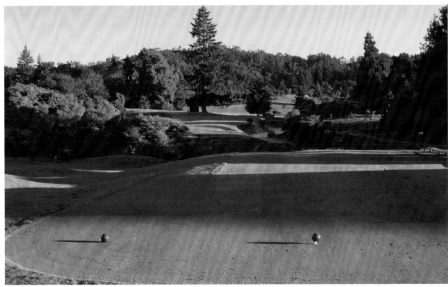

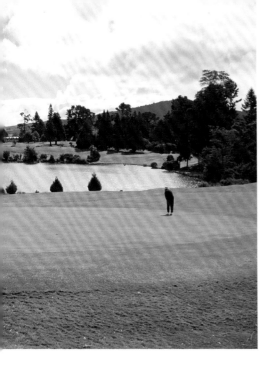

◀ **Surface calm**

Rotorua's striking thermal features seem at odds with its traditional-looking parkland terrain of trees and lakes, which steam in cold weather. Yet below these tranquil fairways there is constant activity. The staff keep a regular vigil for sudden areas of dead vegetation which would indicate a developing underground hotspot.

▶ **Glorious mud** (OVERLEAF)

You'll smell it before you hear it, and you'll hear it before you see it. Rotorua's whiffy boiling mud pools may be hidden away but their presence is constantly felt. Golfers are asked not to retrieve balls from the pits, not only for their safety but to keep its features as unsullied as possible.

On the other hand, your playing experience is suffused by the rotten-egg smell of sulphur – and the smell gets worse in low cloud and damp weather, conditions not exactly rare in New Zealand.

"The locals are immune to the smell," smiles general manager Peter Christiansen. "We don't notice it at all. But it's nothing to worry about. The sulphur in the air is rumoured to be good for your health."

Rotorua is built on pumice, which gives first-rate rapid drainage after rain. It lends the course an all-weather feel, and the holes are perfectly playable just a few minutes after a storm. But despite the firm surface, the ground is constantly shifting because of underground thermal activity – although the members only notice changes over a period of years. Not surprisingly, the humps

and bumps this activity creates have given the course a links-like appearance.

The dynamic nature of the thermal zone keeps the greenkeepers on their toes as it must be constantly surveyed. They monitor the ground temperature throughout the course with a special probe, keeping a regular watch for areas where the grass suddenly dies for no apparent reason. This indicates a developing hotspot, and perhaps a new hazard for the golfers.

Despite all the gas, the moving earth and the boiling mud, however, Peter Christiansen says you will only find danger if you go looking for it. "Perhaps the scariest thermal hazard is on the 14th hole, where any tee shot hit left will land up in a colossal thermal crater. But we certainly do not advise golfers to descend into these craters to try and retrieve their ball – it is far too risky. In fact, we ensure that the mud and hot water pools around the course are fenced off so that players do not enter dangerous areas. In any case, all these features are environmentally sensitive and must be preserved in their natural state. The club has an obligation to ensure that they are kept intact for future generations to enjoy."

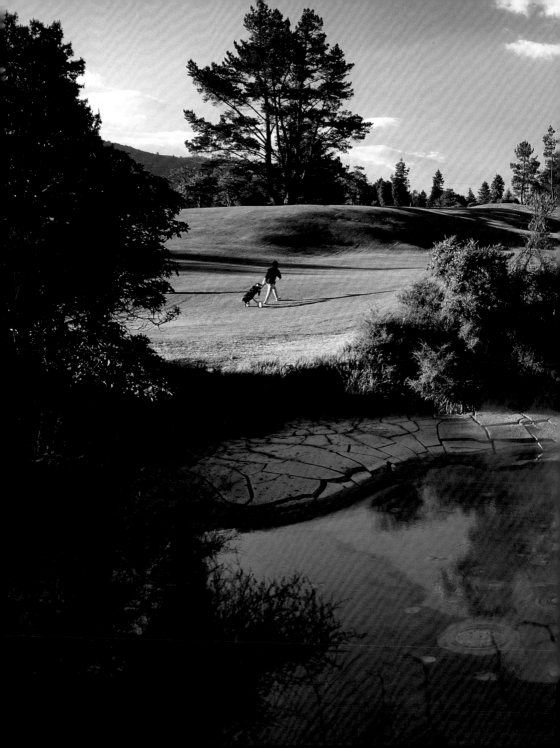

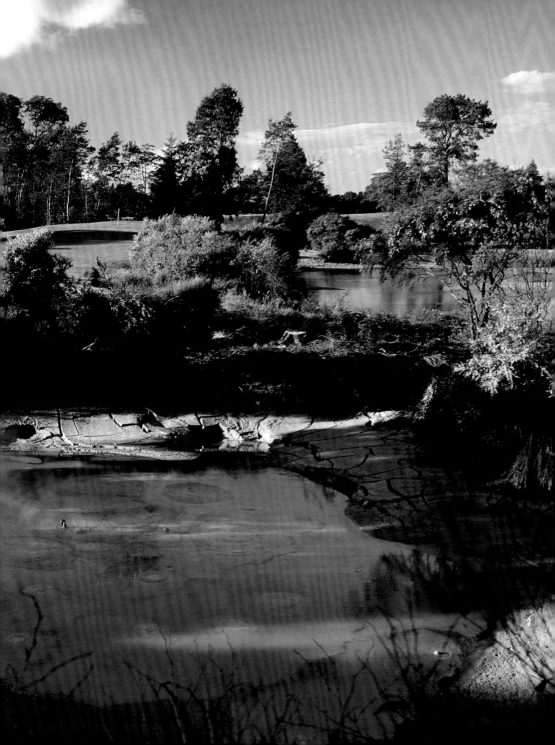

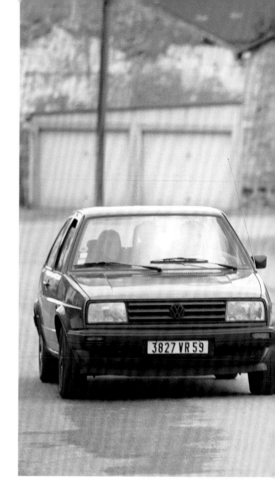

Crosse-Golf

ROUGHING IT
CROSS-COUNTRY

MOST OF US WOULD BE at a loss to know the best
technique for playing the ball out of a pile of cow
dung. But while we were flicking through the rule
book in search of the section on free drops from
bovine faeces, the crosse-golfers of Belgium and
France would be closing their eyes, gritting their
teeth and having a thrash. Crosse-golf is played
cross-country, and the cowpat is just another
tricky situation its players must overcome. Other
common hazards include molehills, barns,
hoofprints, rivers, streams, cabbages, clumps of
nettles and power cables. All crosse-golfers earth
themselves by wearing rubber wellies.

This eccentric strain of golf, also known as
chole, is played by a small but fanatical bunch of
people in the towns of Mauberge, northern France,
and Mons, southern Belgium. The autumn harvest
signals the start of the crosse-golf season, and the
game is played across harvested fields throughout
the winter. Crosse-golfers generally play a course
of nine holes, traversing the hills and dales around
the town. Holes can range between 500 yards
(457m) and 1 mile (1.61km). The target is not a
hole at all but a plank, 7 feet (2m) high and 8
inches (20cm) wide, known as a *planche*.

Mercifully, the game does not require you to
keep score. Before starting each hole, both you and

your opponent must guess how many shots it is
going to take you to hit the *planche*. You then hit
your ball three times towards the target, after
which your rival is allowed to cuff it as hard as he
can in the opposite direction. This manoeuvre,
known as *le dechole*, is of course a major
departure from the traditional game of golf –
although between 1851 and 1856 the rules did
indeed allow a golfer to play his opponent's ball
whenever his opponent declared it unplayable.

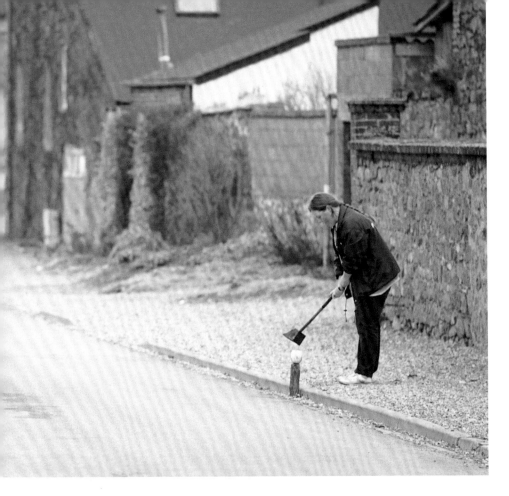

▲ Gutter swipe

Crosse-en-rue, a variant of traditional crosse-golf, played through the countryside, is played through the streets of Hainaut, Belgium, and Avesnois, France. Players normally hit towards beer barrels, positioned near the entrance of the local hostelry.

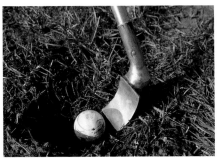

◀ Choosing your tools

The crosse-golf club is also called a "crosse". It has a flat face, known as "le plat" for hitting out of a good lie, and a curved, sharp area for extricating the ball, or "choulette", from the mire. Grips, once made from hemp rope, are these days often made from old bicycle tires.

Just to make things really interesting, crosse-golf is not played with a round ball. The *soule*, as it is called, is egg-shaped, typically measuring 1.6 x 1.8 inches (4.1 x 4.6cm). It is made of wood, usually hornbeam. Players can gain an advantage by using a compressed wood known as *stap*, which has been discovered to give a fantastic spring-like effect. Even then, the longest hitters can slug the *soule* only a modest 150 yards (137m).

The locals have formed a league of 15 societies which compete against each other. Society names include La Renaissance, La Sans Paraille and Les

▼ **French chic**
Crosse-golfers do not have a dress code to worry about and most dress for cold, rain and mud. While carrying five clubs is the norm, there is no limit to how many clubs you can use, other than the size of your bag.

Amis Reunis, but the most formidable is La Societe Joyeuse. Its members are all from the Dausse family, which can claim the greatest ever crosse-golfer, a grandmother named Nicole.

"The best way to play a cowpat lie is to practise on a row of cabbages," she advises. "Only when you have mastered the vegetable patch can you move on with confidence to cow dung."

Her son, Jean-Jacques, is the president of the crosse-golf league. "We love the game," he crows. "No one who plays crosse-golf plays the other golf. That is for bank managers, accountants and people with silly sweaters."

Most crosse-golfers carry five clubs, and very strange implements they are too. The typical *crosse*, which is the name for the club, has a beechwood shaft and an iron head. The head has

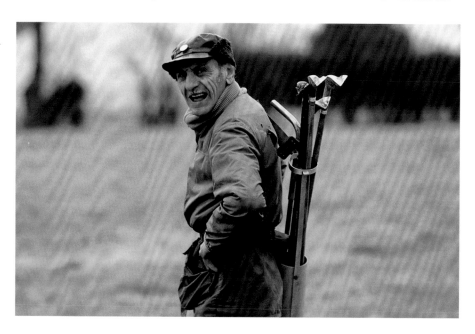

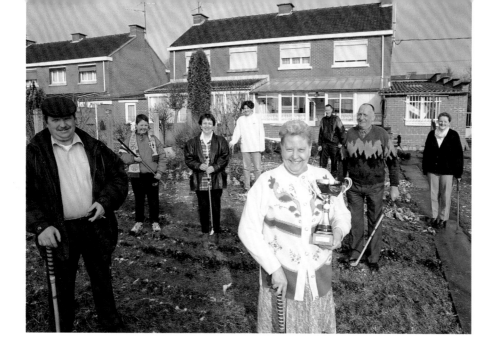

▲ The champion clan
Crosse-golfer supreme Nicole Dausse poses with her family. The Dausse clan form La Société Joyeuse, the best crosse-golf group of them all. Their secret? Practising in the vegetable patch.

two separate parts to serve two distinct functions: *le plat* – the flat part – is designed to drive the ball forwards and upwards in the orthodox golfing manner; while *le pic* – a sharp, curving prong – enables the player to dig his ball out of a poor lie. The grip of the *crosse* was once made of hemp rope, but is now made of rubber or leather.

Although few people outside the region have heard of crosse-golf, the French claim that it is, in fact, the original form of golf. There is evidence that it has been played in France since 1353. The Scots, it is argued, arrived to fight alongside the French against the British at the Battle of Bauge in 1421, and afterwards took the game back to Scotland. This theory is supported by two contemporary Scottish laws that banned popular sports in order to encourage archery practice. The first, passed by King James I in 1424, forbade football but made no mention of golf; the second,

passed by James II in 1457, extended the ban to golf. This suggests not only that golf grew in popularity after the Battle of Bauge, but also that Scotland's gift to golf was little more than the inventing of the hole.

What is certain is that crosse-golf is endangered. The setting up of the crosse-golf league in 1968 marked a modern-day high point for participation, but by 1994 there were only 500 registered players. Today there are barely 100. The annual match between France and Belgium has had to be discontinued as competitors have aged. Without an injection of new blood, crosse-golf will soon be lost to history.

The UX Open

GOLFING UP AND DOWN MOUNTAINS

YOU KNOW YOU ARE in for an alternative golfing experience when you find yourself scooting up to the 1st tee on a ski lift. The UX Open takes mountain golf to another level – literally. The golf course is thousands of feet above sea level, ten holes long and runs up and down the slopes of an off-season ski resort. The grass on the slopes is cut, but you would still label the mown areas unfairways. Hole lengths vary between 90 and 800 yards (82-732m), and par-2s and par-6s are commonplace. There are no greens, merely painted circles 20 feet (6m) in diameter, with flags in the middle. Once your ball lands in the circle, you have completed the hole.

"It's hard to describe the typical terrain of our courses," says the event's American founder, Rick Ryan, "because it is unbelievably different from mountain to mountain. It ranges from weeds, rocks and dirt at Mammoth Mountain in California, to lush grass at Holiday Valley in upstate New York. I would say the fairways are like your back yard on a bad day. The rough is like the worst rough you will ever find on a golf course. The slopes are the biggest hazards. Then you have boulders, gravel and dirt. And, it's amazing how much stuff you find left behind at ski resorts once the snow thaws, from beer cans to skis to poles and hats."

The UX Open is played every summer. There are four qualifying events throughout the States and, at each, 50 golfers compete for three spots in the final. Players start at the top of the mountain and play a course which usually consists of seven downhill holes and three uphill ones. Level par or better tends to give you a chance. In the grand final, the format switches to Survivor-style elimination: one player is knocked out at every hole. The winner receives a red crushed-velvet jacket, similar to those worn by Tower of London Beefeaters.

The UX Open has just ten rules, compared with traditional golf's 34. You are allowed only four clubs, although in truth you wouldn't want to be carrying many more. Also, you are allowed to place your ball within a club's length of where it lies, no nearer the hole. Despite this big advantage, luck still plays a huge part. Adam Kokinda travelled 2,200 miles (3,540km) from Las Vegas to New Hampshire for one of the qualifying events, only to see his first shot smack into a boulder and rebound deep into a forest, never to be seen again. He never recovered from the shock.

Being a great traditional golfer does not necessarily mean you'll be a great mountain golfer. Several club professionals play in the event, but in recent years they have been trounced by 5-handicapper Peter 'Mungo' Shorrey, a guy who spends his life on mountains setting off explosives to trigger controlled avalanches.

"Maybe Peter's line of work helps him in judging mountain distances," says Ryan, "but the

▶ **High slope rating**
Played up and down summer ski slopes, The UX Open has drawn adventurous golfers from all over the United States. If you want to see your ball again, it pays to position a ball-spotter ahead of you.

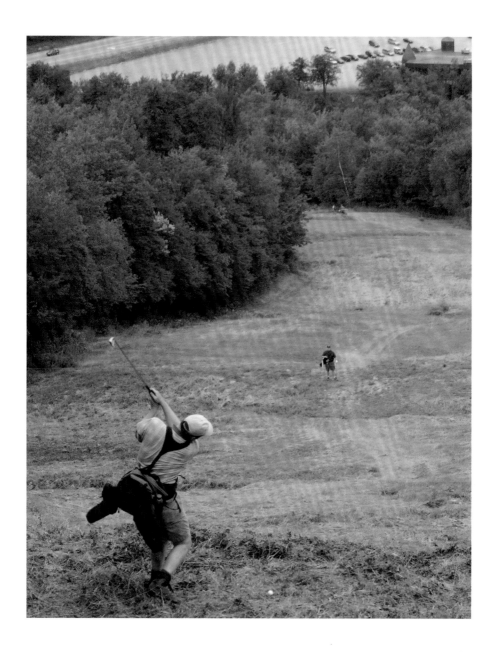

> "Tiger Woods would make a great mountain golfer because he is mega-fit and he has all the shots."

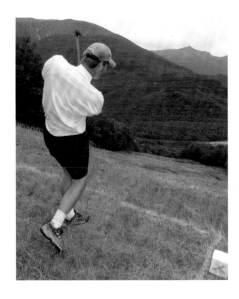

RICK RYAN

main thing is you must be very fit. You also need a lot of shots in your repertoire to deal with all the sidehill lies. You need to know how to play it off your back foot for a downhill lie, or off your front foot for uphill. Tiger Woods would make a great mountain golfer because he is mega-fit and he has all the shots. Someone like Craig Stadler would struggle. He has all the game in the world, but lack of fitness would find him out."

The first UX Open was played in 1999, but the roots of the event can be traced to 1981, when Rick Ryan was at college in Vermont. "I think we'd had a few drinks," he grins. "A group of us decided to climb a nearby peak known as the Snowbowl, about 2,000 feet (610m) high. Someone said: 'Hey, I've got my clubs in the trunk.' So we took them, hiked up the mountain and hit balls around.

"You know that feeling you get when you hit from an elevated tee, and it looks like the ball is never going to land? Well, imagine that same feeling when you're thousands of feet up. It felt like we could hit into the next state. We used trees as targets and invented par-3s and par-4s. We emptied a bag of balls up there."

Despite the buzz Ryan got from the experience, he didn't give it a second thought until 15 years later. The 1990s had witnessed the rise of extreme sports. It dawned on Ryan that golf had become

▲ **Level playing field**

The tee is the one time you can be reasonably assured of a level stance and decent lie. After this you are up against trees, rocks, canyons, scrub bushes and anything else the terrain can throw at you.

more popular with the young, primarily because of Tiger Woods, but also because of Hollywood films such as *Tin Cup*, *Happy Gilmore* and *The Legend of Bagger Vance*. "Golf was reaching a younger audience," he says. "I got to thinking how I could marry up stodgy old golf with extreme sports. I remembered my mountain golf experience in college. When I discovered that there were 300-400 hundred ski resorts in the US that are virtually empty in the summer months, things started to make a lot of sense."

Despite The UX Open's apparent break from tradition, Ryan believes his tournament is very much in keeping with the spirit of golf. "I love the

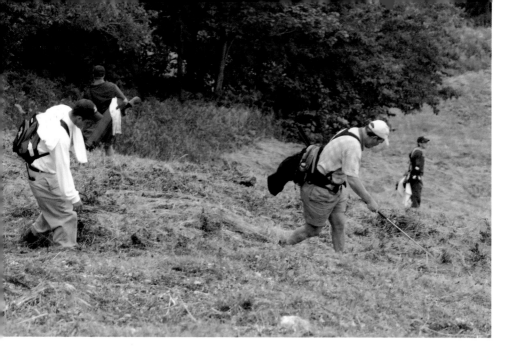

▲ It's a gonner

The event stimulates great camaraderie – you will find
yourself willing to spend plenty of time looking for your
opponent's ball. You do, however, know that on the next
hole you'll probably want your opponent looking for yours.

traditional game, but golf is not about $200
rounds, riding buggies and the length of your
shorts. The essence of the game is the company, the
competition, walking, hitting a ball to a target,
enjoying the outdoors, enjoying a beverage and a
toast at the end – and those are at the heart of The
UX Open. Also, we are using the natural terrain, as
they did in Scotland years ago, before bulldozers.
So as much as this is new, young and extreme,
The UX Open is really kind of a throwback."

Ryan believes his tournament will appeal to
anyone who feels suffocated by the jacket-and-tie
culture of the traditional game. "Some people find
the rules and protocol of golf stringent and

regimented. I wanted this to be very different. We
are not going to tell you what to wear. If you want
to play half naked that's fine with me – though it
would be better if it was the top half. "There's a
picture on our website of two players on a ski lift
with their clubs. One guy has traditional garb, long
trousers, collared shirt and visor; the guy he's
sitting next to has long hair, a bandana, a tank top,
blue-jean shorts and hiking boots. And they are
playing the same tournament at the same time. I
am encouraged by that picture."

The UX Open has gone from strength to
strength, and is even televised in the States. Ryan
believes its success lies in its emphasis on fun. "We
try to stage it at resorts where there is a festival
going on – live music and so on, and we always
have a big party afterwards. The tournament can
also get you on television for your golf skills. When
else are you going to have the chance of that?"

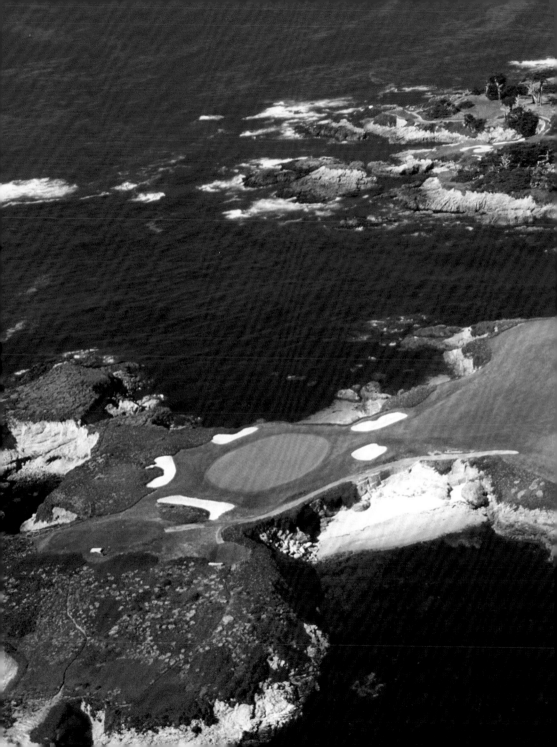

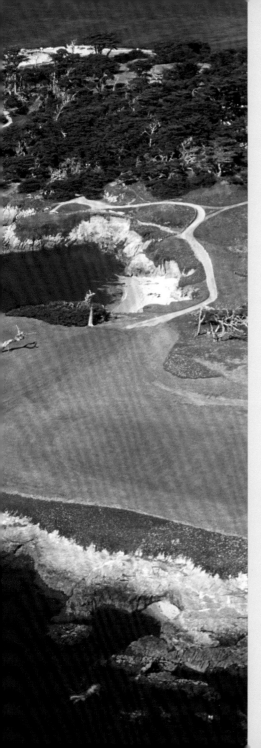

3

Courses for Concern

The dramatic 16th hole at Cypress Point, California, straddles the Pacific Ocean. If golfing on the edge of the ocean isn't enough to fire some adrenalin into your veins then try playing through a fairway of unexploded bombs, or past a volcano due to erupt, or over crocodile pits at the Lost City Course, Sun City.

Kabul Golf
and
Country Club

GOLF IN A WAR ZONE

THE KABUL GOLF AND Country Club is an hour's drive north of Afghanistan's war-torn capital, in a mountainous region known as Qargha Lakes. The only road to it is a pock-marked track through massacred conifer plantations. The visitor's first view of the nine-hole course comes on rounding the final bend. There are no tees, no flags and the

decrepit shell of a clubhouse is full of sheltering goats. Its roof burned out long ago. Yet the land displays the unmistakeable contours of a golf course: several flat areas in the hillside hint at lost green sites, all but obliterated after three decades of near-constant war.

The course was built in the comparative calm of 1971 to cater for expatriates. Back then, Qargha Lakes was a playground for Kabul's well-heeled classes. There was a yachting marina, and the golf course featured groomed fairways and hard-sand greens. Two years later the Afghan Communist Party seized power, and so began 30 years of war, first against the occupying Soviets and then against the Taliban regime which, after taking over in 1994, declared golf to be against the beliefs of Islam. The course became a battlefield – it is now impossible to distinguish its bunkers from the countless bomb craters. One hole was reserved for a tank park, and five Russian 2.8-inch (70mm). Howitzers still stand to the left of the first fairway.

No one is sure when golf was last played here, although Ian Mackley, an expatriate former captain of the club, says play continued during the Soviet occupation. "The Soviet soldiers used to pick up our balls," he says. "We were forced to pass a local rule allowing a free drop when this happened."

The course might have been forgotten completely were it not for journalist Peter Foster, who was in Afghanistan covering the war against the Taliban for the *Daily Telegraph*. He learned about the course from a chance conversation with a

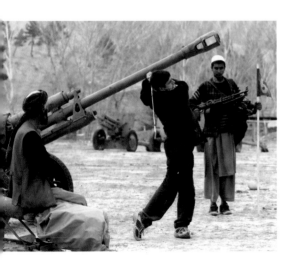

◀ **Forgotten golf**
Golfing at Kabul Golf and Country Club was all but forgotten until Peter Foster learnt about the course while reporting from Afghanistan in 2002. After dusting down some hired clubs, he set about playing a round.

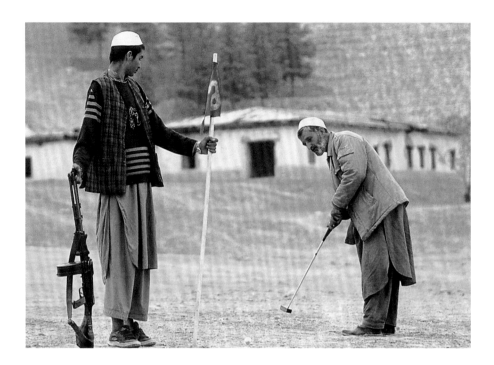

▲ Looking down the barrel

Abdul Qayum (putting) was caddie master and teacher at Qargha Lakes before the Soviets and the Taliban turned it into a war zone. His dream is for the course to be restored to its former glory.

bookshop owner. "The shopkeeper gave me an old guidebook dating from 1976 which had a reference to the course," Foster recalls. "It said the course was at the foot of the dam by the Qargha Lakes boating complex. I'm a mad keen golfer and decided to go and have a look."

Foster and his translator sped off, armed with a hired set of clubs and a dozen ancient Dunlop 65 balls that he'd remembered seeing in Kabul's only sports shop. "The balls had been there since before the Soviet invasion in 1979, and they'd gone lumpy and misshapen" he says. "We took a dozen, and hired the clubs for $50."

They also took along an Afghan soldier as a caddie. His role was to advise not just on club selection, but also on minefield location. "Yes, there was danger," recalls Foster. "Afghanistan is absolutely full of unexploded mines and ordnance – cannon shells, rocket-propelled grenades, PK heavy machine-gun shells. It is lying around by the roadsides, everywhere. You just leave it alone."

The United Nations has branded this area "unstable", but Foster felt reasonably safe as he stepped onto the 1st tee. As well as consulting his caddie, he took into account the advice of several

> "Golf is perhaps a symbol of a settled society and, despite its condition, this course harks back to a time when Afghanistan had that."

Y

PETER FOSTER

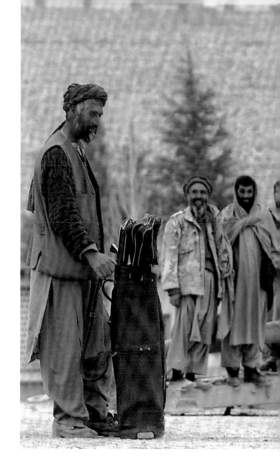

locals who turned out to watch. He could see goats wandering on the course, unharmed. He also noticed a road running across, clearly in use, and resolved to stick close to that.

Foster's tee shot, the first shot at Kabul Golf and Country Club since who-knows-when, was painful. "It was freezing and there was a 30-knot wind blowing," he says. "The ground was frozen and compacted – a dry, dusty moonscape. I had to knock the tee peg in with a rock. I hit a 6-iron. At impact it felt like someone had put 50 volts up my arm. All the bounce had gone out of the ball, and it was like hitting a pebble. It didn't go very far."

Unfortunately for Foster, the 1st hole slopes right-to-left, and his ball pinged off the frosty crust towards those howitzers. Making his way along the hole, Foster tried to work out the layout of the course. He did not find it easy, although one now-dry water hazard was clearly discernible on what he estimated to be the 4th. Looking up, he was extremely perturbed to see an Afghan gentleman bearing down on him. Alarmingly, the man was wearing a black turban – often a mark of someone with a militantly anti-western perspective.

But Foster was in luck. Thankfully, the man introduced himself as Abdul Qayum, Kabul Golf

▲ **Two-shot penalty**
The barrel of a Russian Howitzer shows you the line on the first hole at the Kabul G&CC. No one seems to know whether or not you get a free drop if your ball runs up against them – it is best to just do as you are told.

and Country Club's caddie master. "He couldn't believe we were playing the course after all these years," says Foster. "Astounded, he looked at us as though we were apparitions and he began to show us around. Then suddenly, he smiled and said in English: 'Keep your head down.' That was the only English he knew."

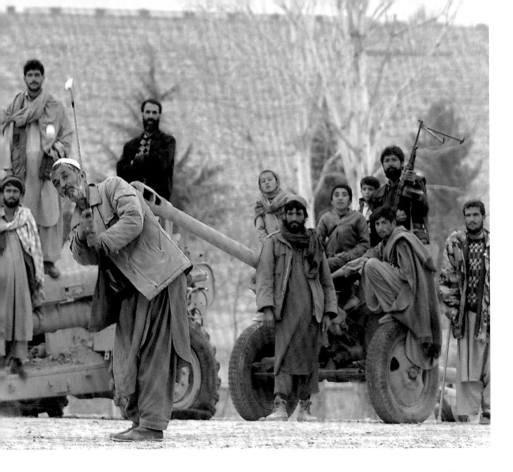

Foster completed his game unscathed, his round yet one more example of the madness that drives golfers to play in ever more extreme circumstances. "Why did I do it?" he ponders. "I'm golf mad. My version of heaven has golf in it. But also, there hasn't been time for frivolous western pursuits like golf around here for many years. Golf is perhaps a symbol of a settled society and, despite its condition, this course harks back to a time when Afghanistan had that."

Abdul Qayum's parting shot to Foster was a request to return and rebuild the course, but Foster thinks there are more pressing concerns. "People are starving here. There's been a drought for five years. It would be great to renovate the course, but maybe in 50 years' time."

> ## "The Soviet soldiers used to pick up our balls... We were forced to pass a local rule allowing a free drop when this happened."
>
> IAN MACKLEY

Hans Merensky Country Club

SAFARI GOLF

EVERY MORNING, JUST AFTER DAWN, a 4X4 jeep appears on the 18-hole championship course at the Hans Merensky resort. Behind the wheel is Andre Welgemoed, head of security. His job is to clear the course of wildlife, and he has his work cut out. The holes run alongside the mighty Kruger National Park, perhaps the world's premier wildlife haven, and Andre can confidently expect to see lions, water buffalo, impala, baboons, warthogs, crocodiles, hippos, elephants and giraffes roaming the fairways. There are also three deadly snakes, the most common of them the Mozambique spitting cobra which can spew venom with dead aim from a distance of up to 8 feet (2.5m).

"If I see a lion I must chase it a good 2 miles (3.2km) from the course," says Welgemoed. "At 2 miles (3.2km) it is reasonable to assume that it won't come back during the day. The best method is simply to make a lot of noise, shouting and beeping the car horn. Lions don't like that."

Welgemoed has had a couple of close shaves while sweeping the course. He once came across a giraffe caught in the fence that separates the course from the Kruger Park. He managed to free it, whereupon the crazed beast charged at him. Fortunately Welgemoed managed to flee into a small bush that the giraffe couldn't penetrate. He has also been chased by a water buffalo which he reckons was just 6 feet (1.8m) behind him when he reached the sanctuary of his 4X4.

Clearly, golfing at the Hans Merensky Club is no ordinary experience. Before being allowed to play you must sign a disclaimer, indemnifying the resort against any mishaps you might suffer at the claws of a wild animal. You are not allowed on the course before 7am or after 4.30pm as animals come out to feed at dawn and dusk. But despite all this, golfers flock to play here.

"Our guests find the experience amazing," says general manager John Creaven. "The danger is the chief attraction. Although we aim to keep the truly dangerous animals away, the ranger is happy for golfers to play around giraffes, impala, warthogs, monkeys and baboons. To play among such creatures is a very exciting prospect: it certainly doesn't seem to put people off."

The 4th tee is only 44 yards (40m) from the Kruger Park's electrified fence. The local authorities like to preserve the natural movement of the wildlife as much as possible, and have built small barrel-shaped holes, known as a cradles, at various points along the barrier. These cradles allow smaller animals, including lions and cheetahs, to get through to the course. Many take up the option because water hazards and lush

▶ **Tough tusk master**
Warthogs make the greenkeepers' lives a misery, as they use their tusks and teeth to root through the grass. Since warthogs are strong and can be aggressive, the staff chase them away with buggies and bikes.

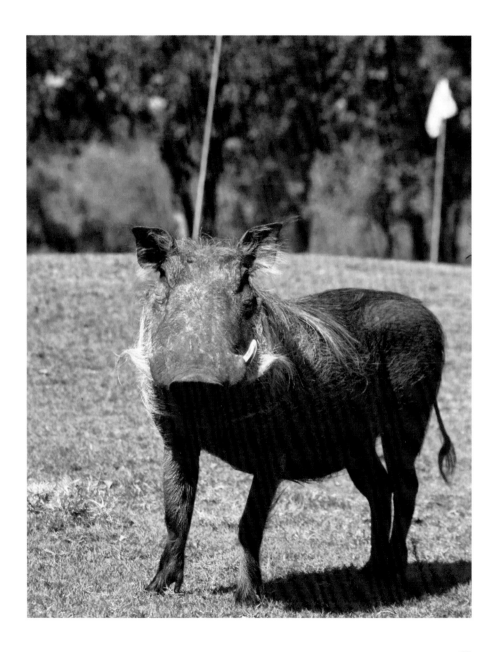

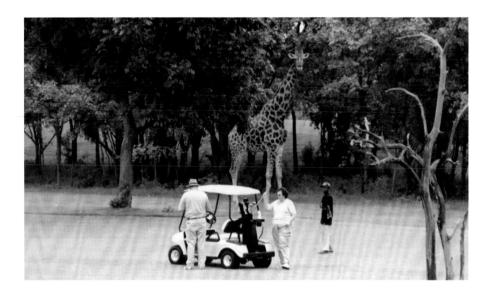

grass make the environment appealing to their prey, including waterbok and impala.

The fence tends to keep the bigger animals off the course, although elephants have found a way to break through. "They place their babies against the fence," explains Creaven. "Their skin is too tough for the electricity to have any effect. They then form a kind of scrum around them and push."

This happens rarely, and elephants are irregular visitors. Even so, an elephant was responsible for the course's one and only fatality. In 1999 a woman was killed after trying to take a photo of a mother elephant with her calf. "Elephants mock-charge," says Creaven, "that is, they run at you then back off. The elephant did this three times. The fourth time, she didn't back off. We stress to all our guests that they must never think of these animals as pets or in any way tame. They are wild animals and you are in their domain."

But although the fence might hinder animals from entering from the park side, Hans Merensky is surrounded by nature reserves and game ranches, not to mention the spectacular Oliphants river. There have been a couple of recent scares caused by aggressive water buffalo, which appear from the nearby Cleveland nature reserve. When a dangerous animal is spotted on the golf course, word gets around very quickly (all the green staff have radios) and the fairways are evacuated within 20 minutes. Dangerous animals are generally tranquilised with a dart and carried away, although staff carry .44 magnums as a last resort.

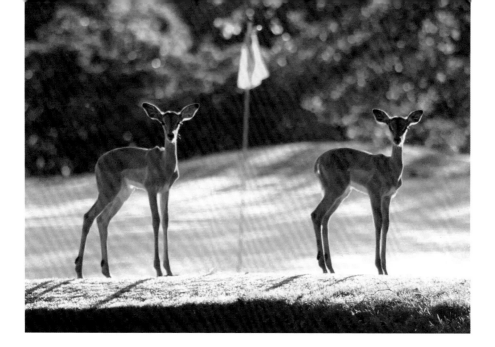

▲ **Safety in numbers**

These baby impala are some of the many grazers tempted to the course by the lush grass. But these animals are stalked by lions and cheetahs. Much of their hunting goes on at night, and golfers are not allowed on the course after 4.30pm.

The animals also keep the greenkeepers on their toes. There is a hippo pond on the 17th hole, and although its occupants stay in the water all day, they come out at night to munch the lush fairway grass. Hippos have no respect for bunkers, and green staff regularly have to sort out the mess they leave. Then there's the impala, which has an uncanny habit of planning its escape route across greens. Staff have grown adept at smoothing out the hoofmarks left by a midnight chase. But the greenkeeper's biggest nightmare is the warthog, which has long sharp teeth that digs up the grass. It is not uncommon to see a greenkeeper chasing one off the course on a quad-bike.

Mobile phone theft is also on the increase at Hans Merensky, thanks to its monkey population. These critters are so cunning that they will wait for you to leave your buggy to play a shot before jumping out and raiding what they can from the cart. John Creaven recently saw one running off with his cellphone, and started to give chase. "Fortunately he dropped it before he got a chance to ring anybody," he laughs.

The course itself is challenging and extremely pretty, a parkland-style layout with plenty of trees and lakes to hit your ball into. The most eyecatching of these is on the signature hole, the par-3 17th. Your tee shot must carry 130 yards (120m) over a lake shared by hippos and crocodiles. Although this pond is a magnet for golf balls, nobody seems to go down there to retrieve them. "Or put it this way," grins John Creaven, "I've never met anyone who has."

Ko'olau Golf Club

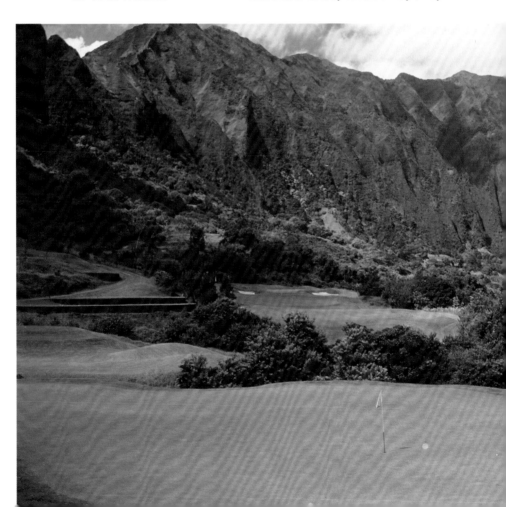

THE HARDEST COURSE
IN THE WORLD

THEY TALK ABOUT TWO course records at Ko'olau. The first is the lowest score from the formidable back tees, an eye-catching 67 by the American PGA Tour professional Dean Wilson. The second, discussed with even more reverence, is the greatest number of balls lost in a single round. This stands at a jaw-dropping 63 and the record-holder remains, understandably, anonymous. "He didn't give his name," grins general manager and PGA pro Rob Nelson. "But he came in off the course three times to stock up on balls in the pro shop."

Since its birth in 1992, the 18-hole layout at Ko'olau has steadily forged a reputation for being the world's hardest. Until recently its slope rating – the American measure denoting a course's degree of difficulty – weighed in at an unofficial 162. It was unofficial because the rating system only goes up to 155. America's other famed difficult hotspots – Pine Valley in New Jersey and Augusta, Georgia – are ranked at just 153 and 152 respectively. The Ko'olau course has since been softened, with 15 bunkers taken out and

the jungle cut back, but it still represents a bone-chilling test of golf.

What makes the course so tough? First, it is carved through spectacular but deadly rainforest, and impenetrable undergrowth flanks the fairways – anything miscued is lost. Second, the holes are constructed over a series of ravines that have been chiselled out by rain running off the slopes of the 2,000 foot (610m) Ko'olau Mountains. A round off the 7,310-yard (6,684m) back tees demands no fewer than 14 carries over these gruesome gorges, some up to 200 yards (183m) long.

What is more, the course is built on the lower slopes of the windward side of the mountains, which makes for awkward stances and awesome gusts – 40mph (64kph) winds regularly whistle across the fairways. The mountainous terrain ensures considerable rainfall, which means that there is actually little or no run on the fairways. Finally there are 109 bunkers, some of them huge, prompting the members to crack stern-faced jokes about there being more sand here than on nearby Waikiki Beach at low tide.

"Off the back tees this is a 100 per cent extreme challenge," says Rob Nelson. "It is so hard that we tend not to use the very back tees as play grinds to a halt. People just cannot get around. I would call it a check-off course for the serious golfer, one you just have to play to tick off your list."

Yet even on a course of nightmare shots, the 18th hole stands alone. It is a 476-yard (435m)

◀ **Gusts and guts**

Ko'olau means 'windward', and on Hawaii, where you are bang in the middle of a 10,000 mile-wide (16,090km) Pacific Ocean, the wind is not to be taken lightly. The course is built on the windward side of the rugged Ko'olau Mountains, and so gains no protection from their mighty slopes. Golfers must tough it out in the gales.

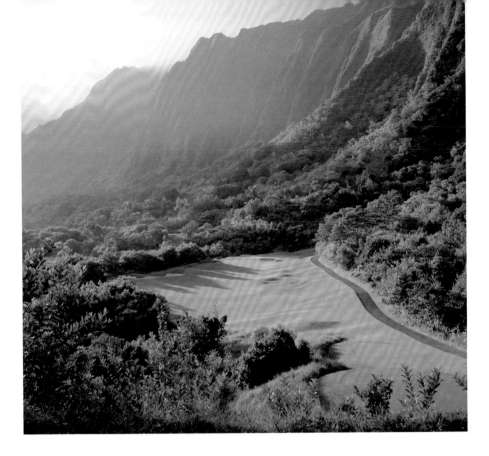

▲ **Fairway to heaven**

If you miss Ko'olau's slender fairways you can say goodbye to your ball. The surrounding thick jungle eliminates any chance of playing a recovery shot. The layout may look like Eden but for golfers trying to score it's a lot closer to hell.

par-4 that doglegs at right angles 220 yards (201m) from the tee. You must carry your drive 200 yards (183m) to overcome the meandering ravine that crosses the fairway in front of you. If you manage it, your joy will be cut short by the sight of the same ravine coming back in front of the green. You'll need another 200-yarder (183m) to clear it a second time. The hole is flanked by 100-yard (91m) bunkers on both sides of the fairway.

Robin Sieger, of the Awesome Eight Golf Challenge, will never forget playing the 18th here. "I hit a ball into the woods off the tee. I thought I would see if I could find it. I walked 20 yards

(18m) into the jungle and found about 50 balls within 10 feet (3.04m) of each other. None of them were mine."

Lost balls are an occupational hazard when playing this course. There are countless tales of golfers running out of ammunition, and the rule of thumb is to bring as many balls as there are shots in your handicap – although that would have been

"This is one of golf's ultimate challenges, and if you're a real golfer you've got to try it."

ROB NELSON

no use to our unidentified record-breaker. Most visiting societies offer a special prize for the player to lose most balls, and nobody is quite sure whether the club was joking when it talked, recently, about building golf ball vending machines on each tee.

"Sometimes people don't want to play here because they feel they will lose a dozen balls," says Nelson. "They see it as 30 bucks down the drain, but you will almost certainly find as many as you lose. We do not send people out to collect them. The course is friendly that way."

Only one tactic will spare you from complete humiliation at Ko'olau, and that is to play off the forward tees. It instantly takes away the need for you to hit your ball over half of the ravines. But if you want to go all the way back, you'll need length and the ability to hit towering long irons in to well-protected greens. You'll also need well-honed course management skills to negotiate the many lay-ups required.

Despite the golfing nightmares it induces, the course is utterly beautiful. At some stage during the round you are sure to find your ball lying next to a wild orchid. There are 500 foot (150m) waterfalls, as well as wonderful views of the azure Kaneohe Bay. The air smells of ginger blossom, and most of the time you can hear the song of the shama thrush. So as the course

▶ **Pond skirters** (OVERLEAF)
There is only one water hazard on Ko'olau, a pond fed by rain running off from the 2,000-foot (610m) Ko'olau Mountains. To add to the overall difficulty of the course, the staff appear to have developed an unhappy knack of placing each flag in an impossible position.

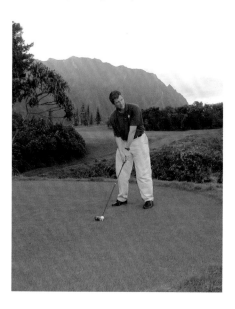

▲ **Driving ambition**
Robin Sieger, of the Awesome Eight Challenge, tackled Ko'olau in 40mph (64kph) winds off the back tees. His score remains a mystery, but much of the time in his five-hour round was spent looking for balls.

batters you into submission, it is vital to get your chin off your chest and drink in the gorgeous surroundings.

"Don't come here to try to score," recommends Nelson. "Come to enjoy the experience and laugh with your mates about the lost balls. This is one of golf's ultimate challenges, and if you're a real golfer you've *got* to try it."

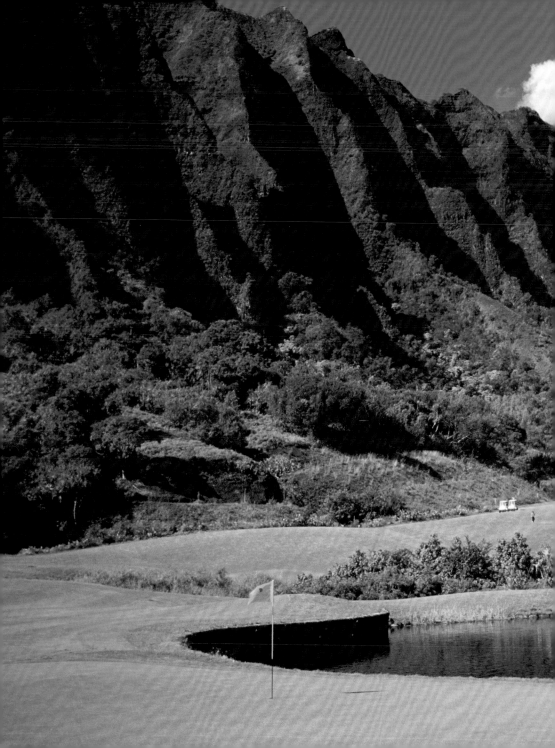

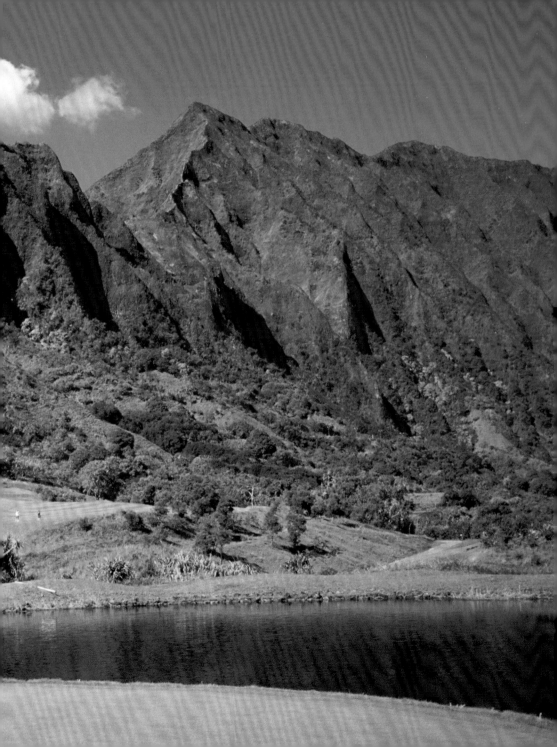

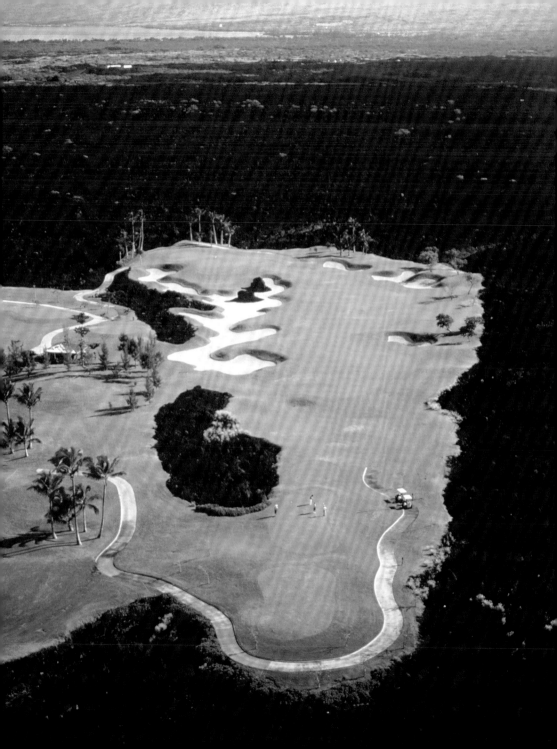

The Waikoloa Resort and The Volcano Golf and Country Club

Y

GOLFING IN THE SHADOW OF THE WORLD'S BIGGEST AND MOST ACTIVE VOLCANO

THE TWO COURSES OF the Waikoloa Resort, on the west coast of Hawaii's Big Island, are sculpted out of lava flows from the world's biggest volcano. Mauna Loa is 13,677 feet (4,168m) high and overshadows the resort. It has erupted 15 times in the last 100 years, most recently in 1984, covering more than 300 square miles (777sq km) of the island in lava. On average, it erupts about every 20 years: scientists say she is swelling right now.

Arnold Okamura, deputy scientist in charge at the Hawaiian Volcanoes Observatory, is monitoring the situation carefully: "There is some activity on

◀ Petrifying drive
Mauna Loa's lava has reached the west coast five times, and Waikoloa's courses are hewn from the black stuff. The 5th hole on the King's course is a driveable par-4, but error will see your ball crashing about in the frozen ancient flows.

Mauna Loa and an eruption will probably take place at the summit. We don't know which way the lava will flow, but Mauna Loa tends to vent south-west and north-east. Golf courses on the west coast of the island are probably in the most danger. Five previous eruptions from Mauna Loa have reached the west coast."

Waikoloa's courses are visually stunning, the black lava along their fringes contrasting with green fairways and the blue Pacific Ocean. Your consolation for hitting a wild shot is seeing your ball ping about in the ebony lava chaos. Sometimes it will even ricochet back to the fairway.

Even though the courses lie in the middle of an old lava flow, the folks at Waikoloa believe there is only a remote possibility of their being affected by a new eruption. They have no emergency warning system, as they know the observatory will give them plenty of advance notice.

"No eruption has reached these parts for 200 years," says head professional Ross Birch. "Also, Mount Kilauea to the east has been erupting since 1983, and I've been told that as long as Kilauea keeps going and there is some release for the lava, the likelihood of a large flow out of Mauna Loa is reduced."

Just as well, because golf courses and lava do not mix well. When lava flows across vegetation it causes it to burn. This creates methane gas which, in turn, fills underground "lava tubes". When the methane ignites, the ground explodes in front of the advancing lava flow, blasting rocks in all directions. Volcanic fumes contain hydrochloric acid, sulphuric acid and glass particles.

The aptly named Volcano Golf and Country Club, 30 miles (48km) east of Waikoloa, appears to be in an even more precarious location. To play its

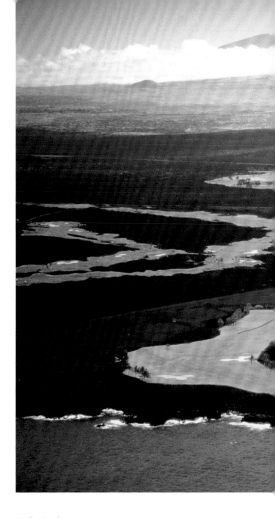

> "The only danger would come from an explosive blast. That could fire rocks and debris far enough through the air to reach the course, and send a huge cloud of ash up into the air."

Arnold Okamura

18 holes is to run a geological gauntlet between earth's most massive and most active volcanoes.

Mauna Loa is 16 miles (26km) west of the course, while literally across the road from the 1st tee is the bleak blackness of the Kilauea Caldera, legendary home of the Hawaiian fire goddess, Pele. Kilauea has been erupting continuously since 1983, and has blown its top 34 times in the last 50 years.

You might assume such a state of affairs would concern Sanae Gathright, general manager of The Volcano Golf and Country Club, but it clearly takes more than impending volcanic catastrophe to faze her. "We don't really think too much about the dangers," she shrugs. "Volcanoes are a way of life for Hawaiians. We have plenty of real, day-to-day problems to deal with at the golf club."

Another reason for Gathright's unruffled attitude may be the charmed life her golf course has led. The course was built in 1921 and, despite its perilous location, its fairways have never once been hindered by a cinder. In fact, there is an old saying here that lava wants to get to the sea as fast as possible. This does seem to be true because Kilauea, on the east side, vents

▲ **Sleeping beauty**
Mauna Loa (Long Mountain) is 60 miles (97km) long and 30 miles (48km) wide. The biggest volcano in the world, it makes up half of Hawaii's Big Island and overshadows the Waikoloa resort on the west coast.

to the east while Mauna Loa, more to the west, tends to vent to the west, which means that between the two is perhaps the safest place to be. "I think Pele must be a golfer," laughs Gathright.

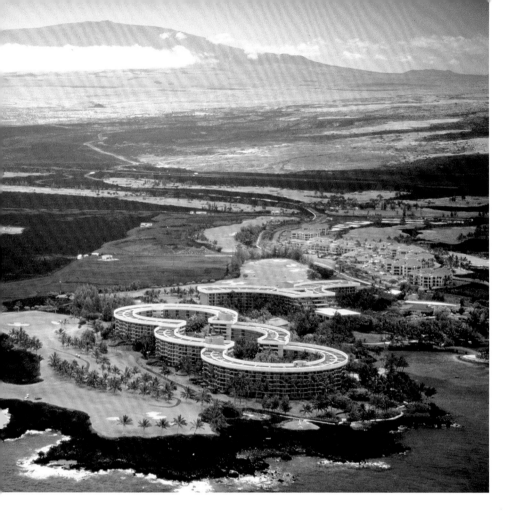

"The Volcano golf course may be within 300 feet (90m) of Kilauea, the most active volcano in the world," confirms Arnold Okamura, "but in fact it is not in too much danger. For a start, the course is 4,000 feet (1,219m) above sea level – a little higher than the main crater. It is certainly above Pu'u o'o, the active vent that has been erupting since 1983. So unless lava suddenly learns to flow uphill, the fairways will not be touched.

"The only danger would come from an explosive blast. That could fire rocks and debris far enough through the air to reach the course, and send a huge cloud of ash up into the air. But there have only been two explosive blasts in recent history, in 1790 and 1924. That's why you see hardened ash around the course, but not really any lava flows."

The Volcano course itself is lush and green, looking a little like Scotland. At this altitude the air

stays fresh even in summer. Copious rainfall means
the course requires no artificial irrigation, although
the ancient porous lava drains the course quickly.
Pitch your ball onto the green and the chances are
it will bound over the back. It is best to run the ball
up to the hole, just like on a Scottish links. The
signature hole is the 17th, a fantastic long par-5,
which you play while gazing upon Mauna Loa and
its enormous twin, Mauna Kea. They are snow-
clad in winter – that is, when they are not erupting.

Playing in such a volatile part of the world has
one other twist. The Big Island of Hawaii
experiences no fewer than 7,000 earthquakes a
year, an average of nearly 20 a day, although only
one in every 35 can be felt. It is not known how

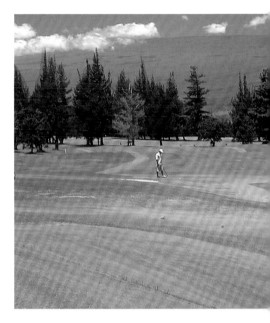

▶ **Mile-high club**
At 4,000 feet (1,219m) above sea level, the air at The Volcano
Golf and Country Club is cool and fresh. The greens are
kept lush by copious amounts of rainfall all year round.

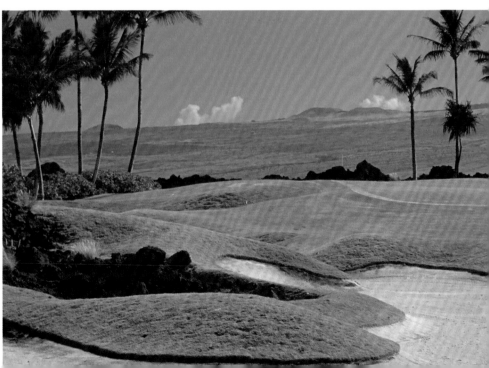

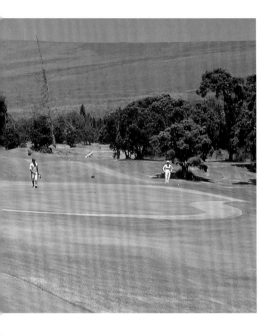

many of those can disturb the roll of a putt, but it makes an exotic excuse for a fluffed three-footer. A large earthquake is often the precursor of a volcanic eruption, so if you feel the earth move on the golf course it might be wise to head for the clubhouse.

None of this seems to bother Sanae Gathright, however: "I guess it is unusual, being next to the most active volcano in the world," she agrees, "but I think that is an attraction for people. Our visitors don't tend to ask about the danger; they just enjoy the course, the scenery and the cooler weather. We have only one contingency plan in the event of a sudden eruption. Run. Run like hell!"

▼ Tricky pitch
Waikoloa's designers – Robert Trent Jones Senior (Beach course) and Tom Weiskopf and Jay Morrish (King's course) – made creative use of the lava, even keeping it in bunkers to intensify the risk/reward elements of their layouts.

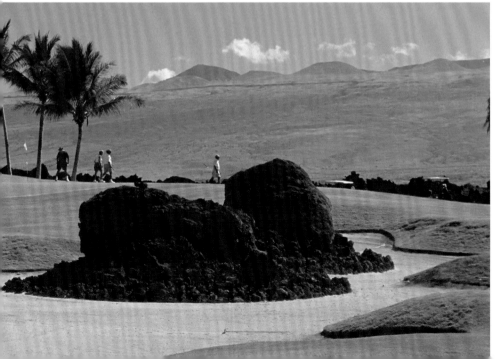

Lost City Course, Sun City

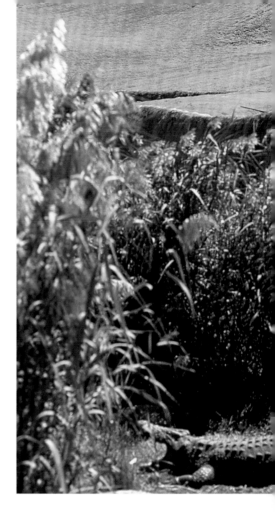

THE 13TH, 180 YARDS (165M) – GOLFING WITH CROCODILES

Having to hit a shot over 24 man-eating crocodiles sounds like the stuff of golfing nightmare, but at the Lost City Course it is no more than the 13th hole. Between the tee and the green of this 180-yard (165m) par-3, there is a deep pit where two dozen razor-toothed reptiles roam. Any tee shot underclubbed or underhit will end up in the croc-ridden chasm. While you are perfectly at liberty to go in there and play your ball, there are plenty of signs around to inform you that you do so at your own risk. It is generally understood that man can outrun these freshwater Nile crocodiles, but it's a high-risk strategy.

To be successful, you must clear your mind of the crocodiles and hit a high, fading mid-iron shot that lands softly on the small green, skillfully avoiding the pit. "People love the hole," says assistant pro Victor Mabule. "You can't actually see the crocodiles from the tee, but you know they are there. It makes the shot much more exciting."

The idea for the crocodile pit came from the course's designer, nine-time major winner Gary Player. "Whenever I design a course, I like to keep as much of the natural flora and fauna as possible," he says. "Of course, there are many crocodiles throughout Africa. The pit also fits in well with the Lost City theme."

Player made the 13th even more distinctive by designing the green in the shape of the African continent, and placing coloured sand in each of the greenside bunkers. "The whole complex at Lost

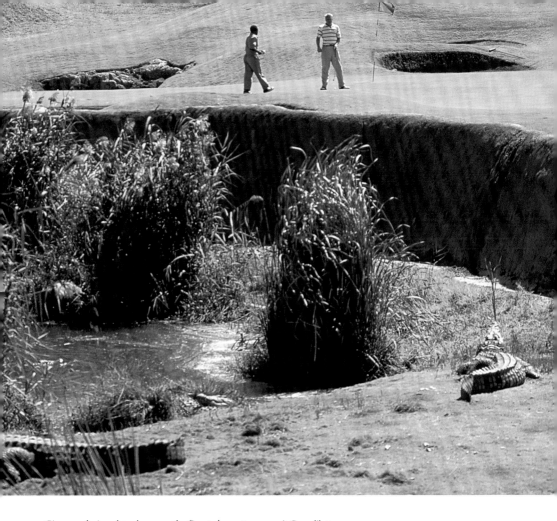

City was designed to showcase the finest elements of Africa," he adds, "and this is why I thought it appropriate to shape the green that way. I hope it will be seen as a sign of respect for this great continent. As for the differently coloured sands, they represent the variety of Africa's ethnic groups, each with a rich and colourful history."

The crocs come from the nearby Kwena crocodile farm, at the Sun City Resort.

▲ **Crocodile tees**

To reach the safety of the 13th green, golfers must play over a pit full of Nile crocodiles. The idea came from Gary Player, who wanted his course to parade the flora and fauna native to the South African wilderness.

The dominant male is 16 feet (5m) long and is known as "Footloose" because his front right foot is missing. The second largest is named "Arnie", after Schwarzenegger, sadly, rather than Palmer.

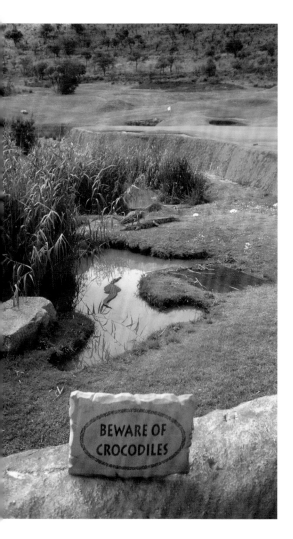

▲ **Anything for a par**

Many balls end up in the crocodile hollow. Its steep sides stop the crocs from getting out, but it is quite easy for golfers to drop down to play their ball back on to the green. Although this is heavily discouraged, the staff have noticed a growing trend for golfers willing to take the risk.

Crocodile expert Brandon Borgelt works at the farm, and enters the fearsome pit at the 13th once a week to check on its guests.

"We currently have five males and 19 females," he says. "They have a social structure, and in the main they co-exist quite happily. The only friction comes during the mating season, from June to October, when the males sometimes fight, and during the nesting season, from September to December, when the females can get a bit uppity with each other. Golfers walking by at these times will sometimes witness a scrap or two."

Mercifully, Borgelt reports that no golfer has been so much as nibbled by the crocodiles. "We mostly feed them on chickens, but try to give them red meat if we can get it. We also use road kill, and even cattle killed by lightning strikes, which isn't as rare as you might think. The other day 13 cattle were killed by a single lightning strike."

Recently Borgelt has noticed a worrying trend with more and more golfers taking their chances in the pit. They may well have been inspired by the Sunshine Tour professional Graeme Francis. During the 2001 Dimension Data Pro-Am, Francis shinned down into the pit, pitched onto the green, jumped out unscathed and two-putted for a bogey four. The sad denouement to this heroic tale is that Francis was later disqualified for his efforts as the tournament organisers had previously passed a local rule forbidding anyone from entering the crocodile hollow.

Borgelt and his colleagues used to retrieve at least 20 balls each on their weekly descent into the pit, but a couple of years ago the balls dried up. Confused, they wondered how the resort's golfers had improved so suddenly and dramatically. Then circumstances forced them to make an unscheduled

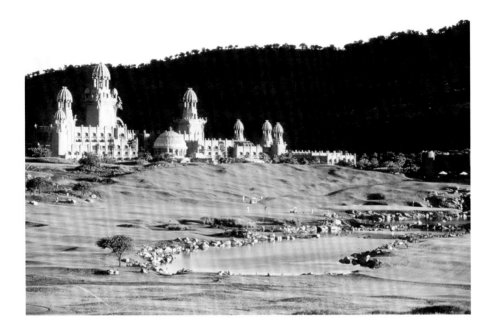

trip back to the 13th. On reaching the pit, they discovered two caddies down there, helping themselves. The caddies later admitted that they had watched Borgelt go in, decided the crocodiles weren't as dangerous as everyone made out, and hopped down to grab some balls to sell.

Borgelt is aware that golf balls rain down on the crocodiles all day, but says that this is not a cause for concern. "Yes, sometimes they get hit by balls, but they are far too tough for the balls to do any damage," he confirms. "They are practically armour-plated – though they can get a bruise if they are hit on the leg. They do, however, get startled by balls landing, and because they are creatures of instinct, the movement of a ball rolling down to the bottom of the pit can spur them into action. They take

▲ **Fantasy golf**
The crocodile hole fits in well with the Indiana Jones-like theme of the Lost City course. The striking clubhouse is modelled on the Great Zimbabwe Ruins, all that is left of the Iron Age capital of the Monomotapa Empire.

a few steps towards it, but as the ball stops moving they back off, almost as if they are not sure why they moved in the first place."

Although Player is extremely proud of all 18 holes on the Lost City course, he has no problem with the crocodile hole stealing the limelight. "These amazing creatures are some of the most exquisite in all of God's creation, and they deserve special attention," he laughs. "The crocodiles add a unique, stimulating element to the course. There's nothing like this sort of danger and excitement during a round of golf."

Kiawah Island, Ocean Course

🍸

SEASIDE STUNNER AMONG MARSH AND DUNE

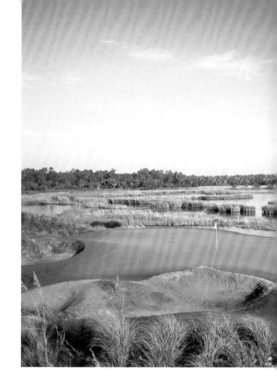

THE OCEAN COURSE AT Kiawah Island occupies a narrow sandbank between marshland and the Atlantic Ocean. Its fairways bob and weave through expansive seashore dunes, skirting lagoons, lakes and marsh as they go. Water comes into play on nine holes. The course measures a chilling 7,937 yards (7,258m) off the back tees, and its slope rating of 155 is the highest possible official figure. A scratch golfer is expected to shoot 79. Small wonder this has been named America's toughest resort course by *Golf Digest* magazine.

But despite the length and the hazards, most Ocean Course veterans argue that the biggest enemy here is the wind. Kiawah Island, 10 miles (16km) long and 1.5 miles (2.4km) wide, runs east to west. It sticks out into the Atlantic Ocean, and the course occupies its south-eastern shore. This singular location means there is no prevailing wind, so golfers can expect to be buffeted from all sides during a round. The course is laid out in a figure-of-eight design, meaning that you will inevitably face shots into

the wind, with it coming off your left and right.

"You can expect a 20mph (32kph) wind here," says Mike Vegis of Kiawah Island Resort. "The fairways are raised to give the golfer a better view of the ocean, but it also makes the holes more exposed. In typical conditions you will see a six-club swing between hitting downwind and hitting into the wind. But you can get 40mph (64kph) gusts, which make things dicey."

Part of the movie *The Legend of Bagger Vance* was filmed on the Ocean Course. The actor Bruce McGill, who played Walter Hagen, fitted in a couple of rounds between shoots. The first day he hit driver, 3-iron to the par-5 16th; and the next day he hit driver, 3-wood, 3-iron. At the 1991 Ryder Cup, the Ocean Course's first major professional event, the wind swung 180 degrees between

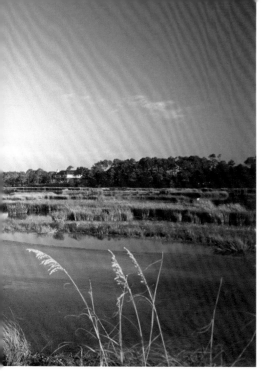

practice and competition. On the 191-yard (175m) 17th, Bernhard Langer went from hitting an 8-iron (with which he managed an ace) to a 3-wood.

Langer's team-mates that year included Mark James, the 1999 European captain. James knows all about what the wind can do. He played in all five series of matches, winning two and losing three, and was 8-over-par when he lost his singles match to Lanny Wadkins at the 16th.

"It was harder hitting downwind than into it," he recalls. "Most of the greens are raised, so you can't run the ball in – you have to pitch it. The greens are firm, however, and the ball usually bounds through.

◄▼ **Lesser of two evils**
In designing the Ocean Course, Pete Dye strove to give the golfer one side of the hole that he could recover from and one side that he couldn't. One of the best examples is the 13th, where water skirts the entire length of the right-hand side of the hole, while bunkers and mounds await up the left-hand side.

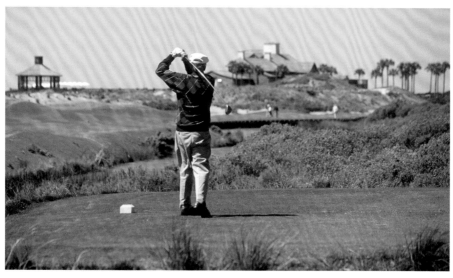

I would try to shape the ball into the breeze to give it a little more softness on landing, but that's not easy downwind. You are always going to miss greens on the Ocean Course."

The spectacular swales are characteristic of the course, and perhaps its second-strongest line of defence. Green aprons are shaved, encouraging your ball to trickle off the putting surface and down severe slopes into bunkers and deep basins known as collection areas.

"Typically you will have two options," advises James. "You can either putt up the sharp bank, hoping and praying that your ball has the right speed to roll down to the hole or you can play a

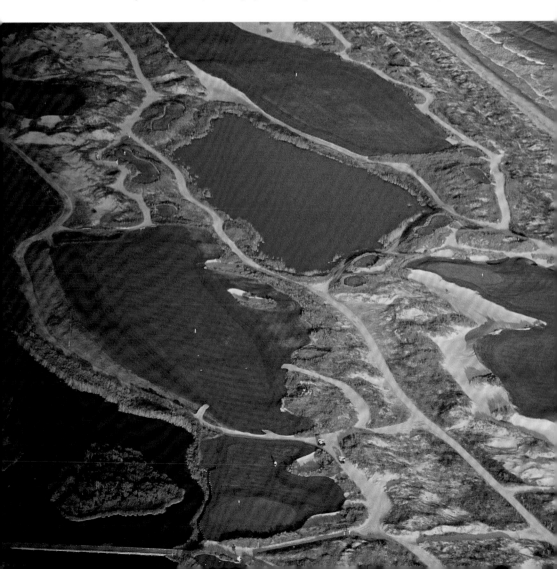

sand-wedge off the back foot, firing the ball into the bank so that it pops up and then checks and dribbles down to the pin. I usually plumped for the latter because that's the shot I resort to when I'm in a state of panic with my short game!"

That's not all. The course's designer, Pete Dye, deliberately sculpted the green surrounds to offer a

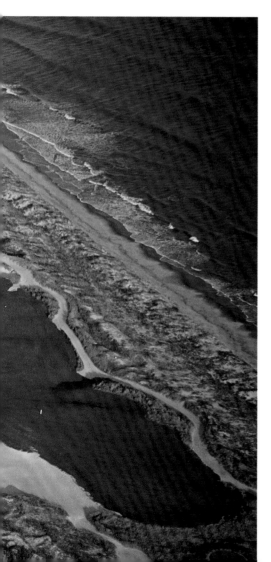

side where you can afford to miss and a side where you can't. "You have to learn the course to know which side is which," says Mike Vegis. "On the 13th hole, for example, it's obvious – there is water all down the right, but you have a chance of an up-and-down if you miss the left side. Elsewhere it is more subtle. On the par-3 14th you have a fairly straightforward par-save from the front right, but if you are left or long of the green, you're dead."

The sheer length of the course from the back tees makes driving a nightmare. Several holes require huge hits to reach the fairway, including a notorious 244-yard (223m) blow across the marsh at the 2nd, and a 212-yarder (194m) over a lake at the 13th. "The fairways are actually quite generous," says Mark James, "but missing them is fairly terminal. It's usually a lost ball, and if you do find it you will probably wish it was lost."

Flanking the fairways are huge, sandy waste areas spiked with wiry dune grass. Your chances of moving your ball from the dune grass are no better than 50-50, and even from a clean lie, a good strike is no cinch. "The sand depth is really inconsistent because of the wind," Vegis adds. "Sometimes you will be hitting off clay-type dirt, at others you're in a deep pile of soft stuff."

So how does one tame the Ocean Course? "It's so visually intimidating that people try to overpower it," reckons Vegis. "My advice is to leave the driver in the bag and play connect-the-dots golf. Even better advice is to swallow your pride and go off the forward tees…"

◀ Atlantic commotion

The fairways of the Ocean Course are generous, but leave them and you are in a dune or marshland. The flatness of the layout meant that golfers could not see the sea so architect Pete Dye had the fairways lifted.

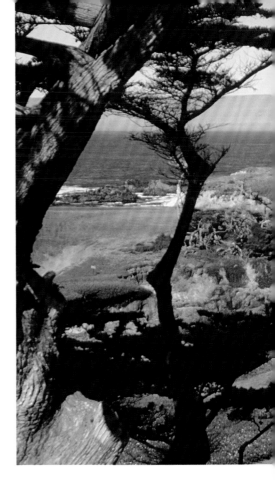

Cypress Point Golf Club

THE 233-YARD (213M) 16TH, THE MOST SPECTACULAR PAR-3 IN THE WORLD

THE ROUTE FROM THE 15th green to the 16th tee at Cypress Point takes you into a narrow avenue of gnarled cypress trees. The avenue takes about 40 seconds to walk through and offers a short-lived respite from the elements, especially the gales that charge in endlessly from the Pacific Ocean. On a more cerebral level, it also detaches the 16th from the rest of the course; you have a few stolen moments of calm to consider the awesome challenge to come. You emerge from the tunnel feeling like a gladiator entering the arena.

The view from the tee can make a pro's knees wobble. Separating you from the green are 220 yards (201m) of tumultuous Pacific Ocean. While surges of salty spray soar from the frothy waves, stinging your cheeks and making your eyes water, above the roar of the wind you can hear seals barking on the rocks below. Their caustic bellowing somehow brainwashes you into ignoring the bail-out area to the left, which exists so that you can play the hole as a par-4. Something deep inside tells you that you've got to have a crack at the green.

To reach and hold the putting surface, you must manufacture a shot in which the ball flies like a missile but bounces like a lump of cheese. You must also remember that you need to allow for the wind, both for its direction and distance. Anything hit with slice or a big hook, or which is too long or too short, will come to rest 20,000 leagues under the sea. As you stand on the tee you can almost feel your clubs shrinking down into your bag, pleading with you to pick one of the other 13 for the task.

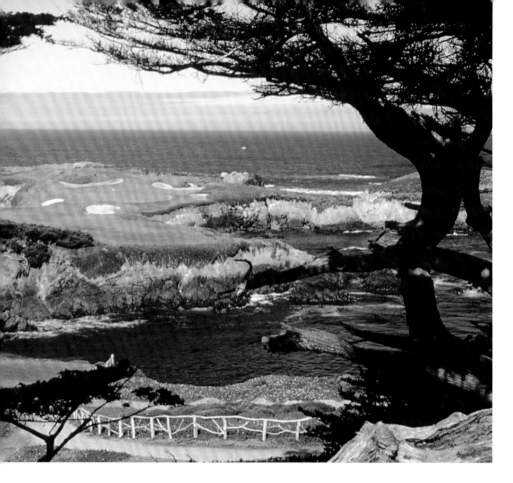

▲ Untamed melody
The 16th hole feels detached from the rest of the course. To hit the green of this long par-3 you must hit a powerful shot that flies high and stops quickly, while allowing for the strong winds buffeting you from the Pacific Ocean.

Head professional Jim Langley has been at Cypress Point for more than 30 years, and tells an interesting tale about the wind here. "Cary Middlecoff, the three-time major winner, was playing here in 1952," he recalls. "When he reached the 16th tee, the wind was so strong he could not get his ball to stay on the tee-peg. He argued that the course was unplayable, but Pebble Beach head pro Peter Hay told him there was nothing in the Rules of Golf to say you had to use a tee-peg. He made Middlecoff hit the ball off the turf."

Golfers have described playing the 16th hole as a near-religious experience. Spookily, the highest tournament score is 16, recorded by the American Ed 'Porky' Oliver; but there have also been 16 holes-in-one. Famous aces were struck by Bing Crosby, in 1946, and Jerry Pate, with an orange ball, in 1982.

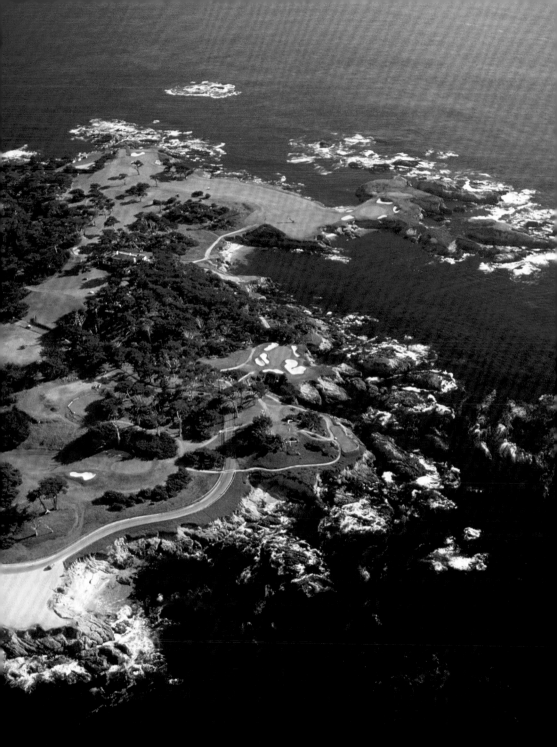

The sheer drama of Cypress Point's 16th has made it perhaps the most photographed and painted golf hole in the world. Acclaimed Scottish painter Graeme Baxter is the latest in a long line of artists to make the pilgrimage. "I would have to say it is the most dramatic hole I have ever seen," he enthuses. "Photographs can't do justice to it; it's more extraordinary than that. For my picture I moved back from the tee to allow myself to include it in the frame, in the foreground. It helps golfers to see what an incredibly challenging shot this is, right across the bay."

Baxter spent two days by the tee, assessing the challenge of the hole and how its look changes through the day. He saw that it was even more spectacular with the tide well in, waves crashing over the rocks, and decided to paint a high-tide scene. "I also wanted to depict a regular day with a bit of wind and swell about," he says, "although I always set my golf paintings on a sunny day. Golfers always remember their best or most enjoyable games as happening in lovely weather." Despite having the course virtually to himself for 48 hours, Baxter resisted the temptation to have a knock at the green. "I was there to work, and in any case I didn't have any clubs with me," he sighs.

Although the course was laid out by Alister Mackenzie, who also co-designed Augusta National with Bobby Jones, Mackenzie himself gave credit for the 16th to Marion Hollins.

◀ **Holy Trinity**

Golfers speak of playing Cypress Point's 15th, 16th and 17th holes in religious terms. Architect Alister Mackenzie once wrote: "The natural beauty is unsurpassed, having awaited for centuries only to have the architect's moulding hand sculpture a course without peer." The ocean claims 1 foot (0.3m) of coastline every year, but the club has built defences to maintain these breathtaking holes.

> ## "I would have to say it is the most dramatic hole I have ever seen. Photographs can't do justice to it; it's more extraordinary than that."
>
> ## GRAEME BAXTER

Hollins was a remarkable woman who won the US Women's Amateur, captained the first American Curtis Cup team, played exhibition matches with Bobby Jones, designed golf courses, played top-class polo and introduced steeplechase to California.

Hollins worked closely with Mackenzie on Cypress Point. Apparently the pair stood on the site of the 16th tee, pondering the route of the hole. Mackenzie envisaged a short par-4, playing out to the left and then pitching to the green. On hearing this, Hollins teed up a ball and sent a soaring shot 219 yards (200m) across the ocean. "Let's put the green there," she said.

The small peninsula that hosts the 16th green takes a severe pounding from the Pacific, which gobbles away up to 1 foot (0.3m) of coastline a year. But Jim Langley says the hole is safe for the time being: "We've built up the greenside defences recently, to guarantee the 16th for another 50 years," he says. "The members here are extremely proud of the hole and are determined to protect it. We've drilled metal bars 20 feet (6m) into the cliff face, added concrete, then had the whole thing sculpted and painted to make it look natural. It's a little like Disney World down there."

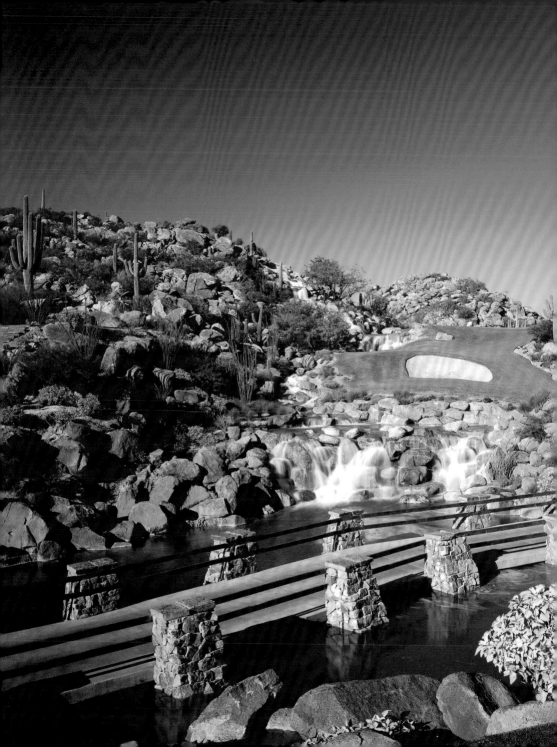

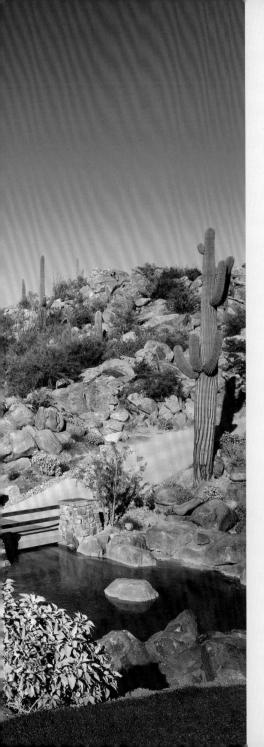

4

Golf by Design

The par-3 6th hole at Stone
Canyon, Arizona, is fighting a
losing battle against the
invading Sonoran Desert.
The hole is a testament to
our ability to fabricate
extreme golf courses;
unnatural, bizarre and even
erotically shaped challenges
await those who like unusual
tests designed by man.

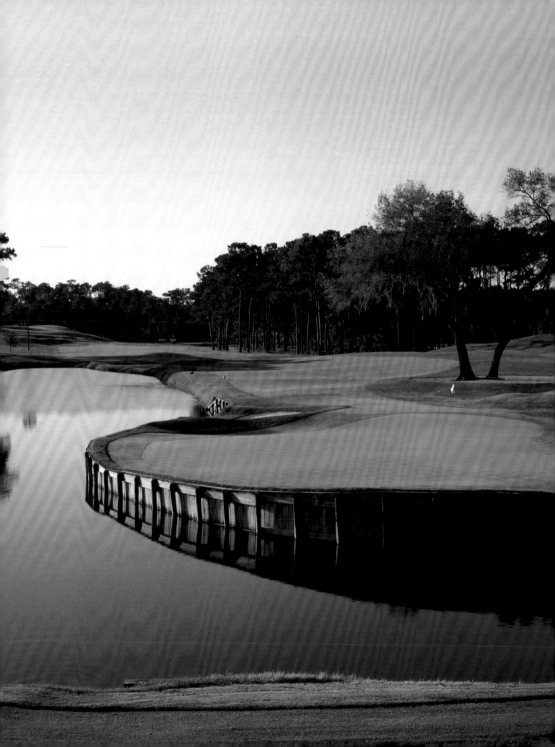

FLORIDA, USA

TPC at Sawgrass, Stadium Course

♆

EXTREME UNNATURAL GOLF

WHILE MANY CHALLENGING courses make use of nature – the terrain, the weather, the flora – maverick golf architect Pete Dye proved that man can set just as stern a test. Dye took a pan-flat goat farm in a north Florida swamp, land so useless that it cost the club only a dollar, and contrived the ultimate target-golf examination. The result is the TPC at Sawgrass, a course where players must plot their way with a surgeon's precision through a synthetic symphony of sand, water and mounding.

Using natural hazards for the course was out of the question because there weren't any – unless you count the alligators. Dye is one of golf's most radical designers, but his reputation for defying convention didn't quite extend to employing

◀ **Man-made marvel**
The Stadium course's bold 16th green bulges out into the lake on land that was once nothing more than a morass. Architect Pete Dye, however, managed to prove that an extensive drainage programme, coupled with some ultra-confident design strategies, can land you a golfing masterpiece on the most unlikely of landscapes.

alligator mississippiensis. Instead, he relied on artifice to make his masterpiece.

His first task was to build massive mounding, the course's most striking unnatural feature. Dye had to drain the swamp for a year before the land was firm enough to drive diggers across. Then he set to work, sculpting spectator mounds and on-course elevation by scooping thousands of tons of mud out of the ground. Aware that the land was still marshy, he shored up many of these newly created slopes with timber. Using wood was a trick Dye had learned from the Scottish courses, and it became his trademark – so much so that some said his courses were in danger of burning down. In any event, the railroad ties at Sawgrass certainly add to its unnatural feel – and also to the target-golf challenge, by visibly defining the hazards.

Dye was not afraid to use straight lines, notably at the 11th green, where the long right-hand bunker is shored up against a lake by yet more wood. But surely the least natural hole is the world-famous and much-cloned 17th, only 132 yards (121m) long but with a surreal island green that rises mirage-like from the middle of a lake.

"Golfers seem to judge the success or failure of their round here by how they played the 17th," says assistant pro Jim Jordan. "It's their benchmark." Statistics suggest, however, that most players leave the course disappointed. In 2002, 122,000 balls were scooped out at Sawgrass, yet only 39,000 rounds were played. That's an average of more than three lost balls per golfer.

Originally branded a gimmick, the hole is now regarded as a masterpiece of modern design, although in fact it came about by accident. Dye's intention was to put water only to the right of the 17th, but as his crew dug, they discovered the earth

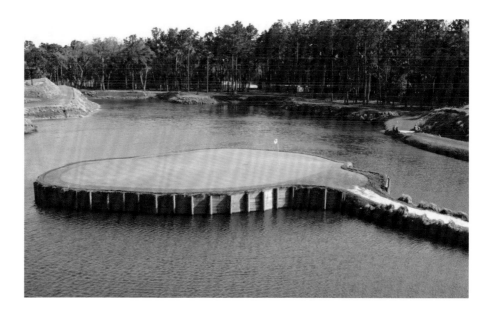

Island greens are now commonplace but the trend began here with the 17th hole – and in keeping with many great inventions its arrival was a fluke. Dye originally intended to place water to the right of the green but an unexpected discovery of sandy soil, perfect for fairways, meant the diggers kept on digging right around the green. The most contrived of holes epitomizes the course's artificial feel.

there was very sandy, and perfect for constructing fairways. More and more earth was excavated to build the 15th and 16th holes, until the only land remaining was the green site.

"I don't think any of us really dreamed up the 17th hole," recalls Dye. "It just kind of arrived. We dug it out trying to get the sand, and actually I think it was my wife, Alice, who came out and said: "Why don't you make it an island hole?"

The 17th illustrates perfectly how the contrived nature of the course sets up an extreme target-golf test, demanding the utmost accuracy in moving the ball from A to B. While building the TPC, Dye gave an interview. "The real trick of golf course architecture," he insisted, "is to lull the golfer into a false sense of security." Yet after playing it, most golfers would conclude that he failed miserably in this aim. The intensely unnatural layout may be enthralling, but there is precious little sense of security to be found, false or otherwise.

Fear strikes you right between the eyes on the 17th tee, but the view down the 18th hole from the clubhouse also lets you know what you are in for. The fairway of this long par-4 is not ungenerous, but is dwarfed by the expanse of water that hugs its entire length. The green is protected by pot bunkers and thick rough, and is angled towards the water. Exciting it may be, but the hole is much more alarming than calming. And so the theme

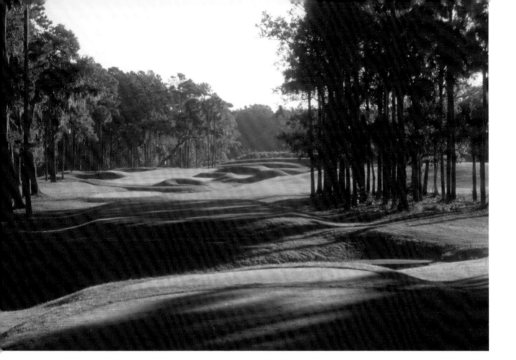

continues for 18 holes. Fairways are squeezed grudgingly between gargantuan bunkers and ubiquitous water hazards. The greens are small, hard and full of acute slopes.

The course opened in 1980 and staged its first Players Championship in 1982, amid a storm of criticism for the design. Some players compared the severity of the layout to a crazy golf course, asking where the windmills were. Jack Nicklaus, who missed the cut that year, remarked that he had never been very good at stopping the ball on the roof of a Volkswagen with a 4-iron. So when the eventual winner, Jerry Pate, threw Dye into the lake by the 18th green, no doubt many of the losers would have liked to throw in a couple of alligators as well.

Today, however, no one has a bad word to say about the course, pro or amateur. A series of minor

▲ **Pot luck**
All gradients on the course had to be constructed, and the sudden appearance of mounding around the greens is characteristic of the course. The pits and troughs on the 8th make finding the putting surface on this long par-3 crucial – especially a deep pot bunker to the left.

▶ **Beat drink and be merry** (OVERLEAF)
The par-5 11th shows the Stadium Course at its most spectacular. Bold lines dominate bunkers and green surrounds. Water and sand to the right of the green force you to hit left, but steep slopes will kick your ball away from the putting surface, leaving you a nightmare pitch.

improvements over the last 20 years has made it more playable, even though it looks as manufactured as ever. "They have done a heck of a job in getting it to where it is now," says Tiger Woods, who won the US Amateur here in 1994. "I've heard stories of how it used to be, but now it's much fairer and a lot more fun to play."

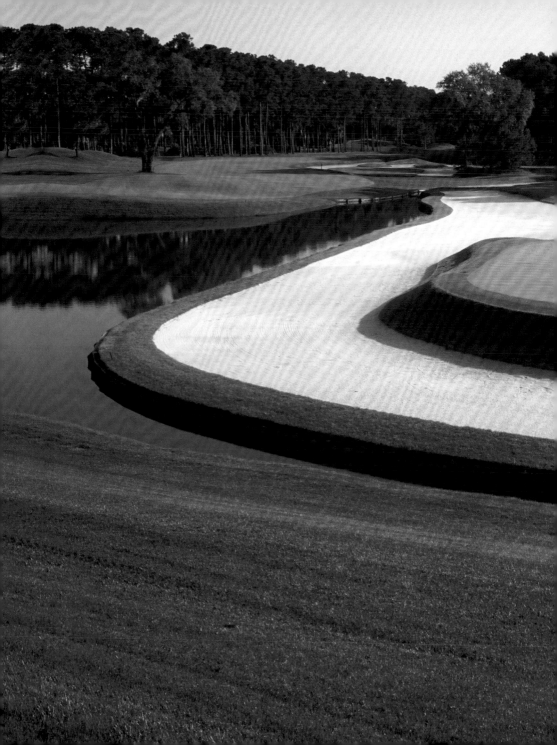

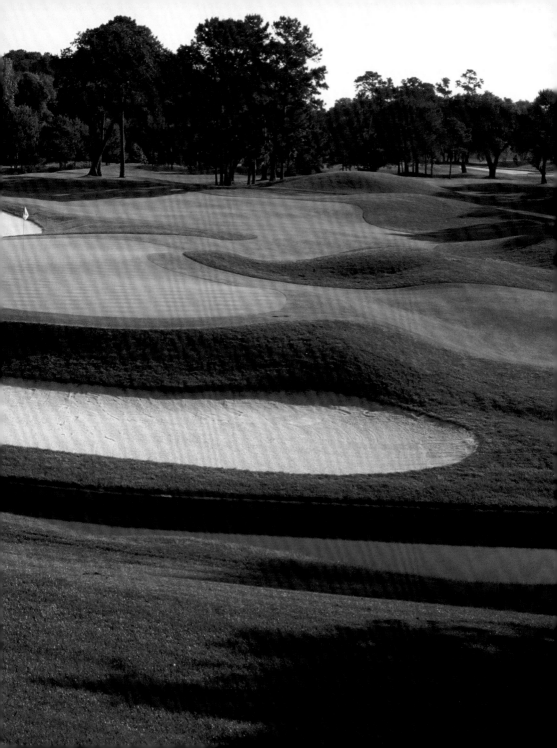

The International Golf Club

BIONIC GOLF AT THE WORLD'S LONGEST COURSE

THE INTERRNATIONAL GOLF CLUB, Massachusetts, is the kind of course that makes you wish you had bought a bazooka instead of a titanium-headed driver. Just looking at the scorecard can make your legs ache – there are six par-5s of more than 530 yards (485m), and two par-3s of over 270 yards (247m). The 3rd hole, a 674-yard (616m) par-5, requires a 260-yard (238m) blow just to reach the ladies' tee. Off the Tiger tees (the very back tees), The International measures a titanic 8,404 yards (7,685m) and has a par of 77. It is without a doubt the world's longest course.

The 4th hole, the shortest of the 18, measures 180 yards (165m). Players need to make the most of it because this is very much the calm before the storm. The course's biggest blockbuster is the 5th, a truly monumental 715-yard (654m) par-6 with a sharp dogleg left. The architect's brief for this hole was that it should never be reached in two.

Originally it was a 680-yard (622m) par-5 but, on the day the course opened, in 1957, local pro Paul Harney, playing an exhibition match, smote two mighty blows to the green. Locals still talk about his second shot, a towering fairway driver which cut the corner, thudded down and trickled onto the putting surface. The course's original owner, a gruff businessman named Burt Suprenant, was furious, and ordered an instant redesign. The hole was extended to 715 yards (654m) and a stand of trees was planted inside the dogleg to eliminate corner-cutting. No one has got up in two since.

The International runs through sandy, rolling countryside, its holes extending between magnificent stands of pine and oak. Despite its extreme length, the fairways are no wider than normal and the bunkering is no more lenient. The man to thank, or otherwise, for this golfing marathon is Geoffrey Cornish, designer of 250 courses across the States and one of only two golf architects listed in *Who's Who*.

"There is no secret to playing The International well," he believes. "All you have to do is hit it long and straight, long and straight all day. It is a supreme test of the long game." Cornish denies the course's genesis was inspired by a pathological hatred of golfers, and instead attributes its astonishing length to owner Burt Suprenant.

"Burt was an eccentric man who rose up in the world very quickly. During the Depression he worked on the government's Works Progress Administration scheme – by 1950 he was one of the wealthiest men in Massachusetts. The problem was that he'd knocked a few people over on his way up,

▶ **Long story**
From the Tiger tees, the 17th on the International Club's Pines Course, is a 440-yard (402m) par-4 with a pond behind the green. Despite a length of 8,404 yards (7,647m) from the back tees, the tree-lined fairways of the Pines are worryingly tight.

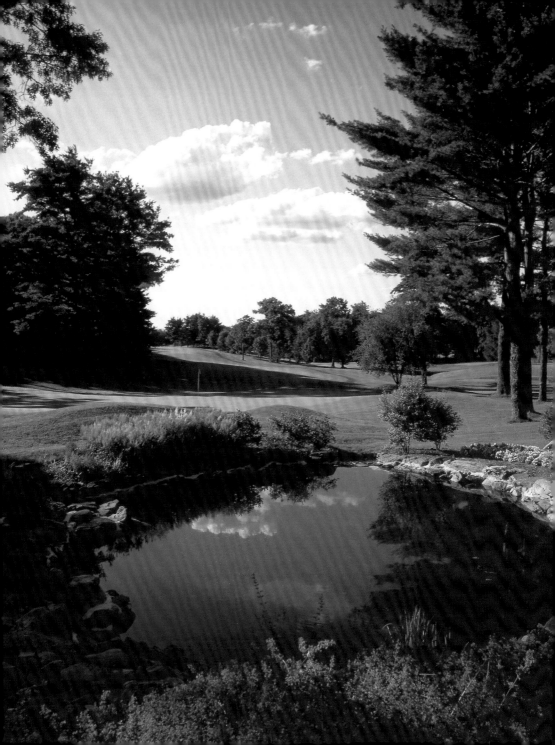

and made himself unpopular. No one would let him into their country club, so eventually he said: 'To hell with this, I'll build my own.' He was no great golfer but he got it into his head that the world's longest golf course would be a great sales point. And he asked me to build it."

Suprenant was proved correct. People turned up in droves to take on the monster, reflecting a curious truth about golfers – that we see exceptional difficulty as a draw rather than a turn-off. "We charged $15 a round back then," Cornish says, "about the equivalent of $150 today. People thought we were crazy, but it was a great success and people came from far and wide to play. There's no doubt about it – golfers just love extraordinary golf courses."

The International is long by today's standards, so it was stupendously long for the 1950s. Cornish admits he had no idea how it might be received, especially after the unimpressed South African

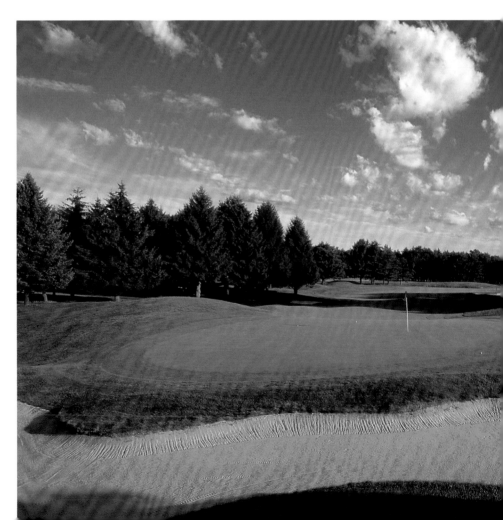

maestro Gary Player said its only challenge was its bombastic length. The designer was buoyed, however, by some kind words from the great Sam Snead, and also by the huge public interest.

"I guess golfers love a stiff challenge for holiday golf or one-off rounds," he says. "But I'm sure country club members would not like the course they play week-in and week-out to be quite so troublesome." His theory is supported by the fact that the members of the International Golf Club

play off tees measuring about 6,500 yards (5,945m).

Despite designing this brute, Cornish admits he has never actually tackled it off the back tees himself. Another golfer never to have played it is Tiger Woods. It's a stirring thought to imagine how the world's most powerful player would handle its longest course – but one that is unlikely to be realised. "I believe they've tried to get him there," says Cornish, "but apparently his fees are a little on the high side." That's Tiger's excuse, anyway.

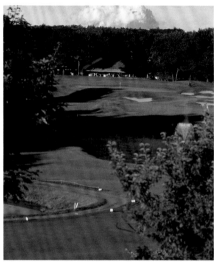

▲ Journey's end

The 18th hole on the pines course measures a healthy 656 yards (600m). A steep hill, massed bunkering and trees do not make your task any easier. Small wonder a scratch player (zero handicap) is expected to shoot 80 round here.

 Small target

At 590 yards (539m), the 11th hole would be a monster for most courses, but here it is only the fourth longest hole. Despite the course's awesome length, green sizes are no bigger than on standard courses.

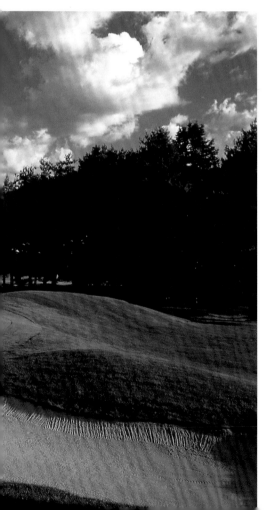

Emirates Club, Majlis Course

LUSH GREENS IN THE MIDDLE OF A DESERT

THE COMPUTERISED IRRIGATION system at the Emirates Club kicks in shortly after dark. At the touch of a button, 900 spinning sprinklers fizz into action. For the next ten hours they hiss water furiously onto the Majlis course, drenching greens, tees and fairways with 1 million gallons (4.5 million litres) of desalinated water. By the time the green staff arrive at sunrise to mow the course, the layout is glistening and moist, and ready to grant another day of awesome desert golf to those lucky enough to have a tee time.

The Majlis course goes by the unofficial name of Desert Miracle. It was built in just eight months in 1987, at the behest of His Highness Sheikh Mohammed bin Rashid Al Maktoum, Crown Prince of Dubai and Minister of Defence for the UAE. Dubai's government has never made it known

▶ Green party
When the desert was first watered, native flora sprung up which had been dormant for years. Now the course's immaculate upkeep has led to it staging one of the European Tour's flagship events – The Dubai Desert Classic.

how much the course cost, but rumour has it that it was about the same amount as the Sheikh earns in four hours.

From the air, the course looks like a giant emerald embedded in the sand, but the man who created it says it is no miracle. "All you really need is adequate water and you can build a course anywhere in the world," says US golf architect Karl Litten, designer of 100 layouts on five continents. "We were very fortunate because we had access to the surplus water from a nearby aluminium plant. At the time, Dubai was desalinating 50 million gallons (227 million litres) of water a day. We needed 1 million gallons (4.5 million litres)."

Despite the challenging environment, Litten recalls few problems during construction. "A course architect loves to get a pure site with no

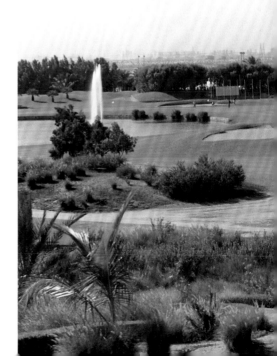

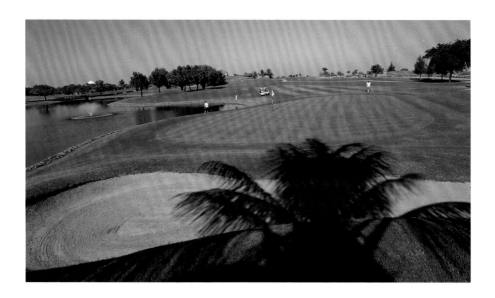

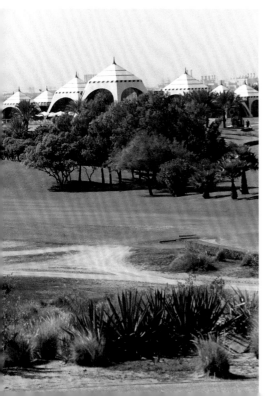

▲ **Hitting the spot**

The Majlis course is a target golf test par excellence. Ponds and bunkers, together with well-watered and receptive greens, encourage you to throw the ball back to the pin.

▶ **Shaping history** (OVERLEAF)

The course rose out of the Arabian Desert in 1987. It was built in just eight months, and at first the greenery took the form of a huge, bizarre square emerald. Further grassing since has diminished the unnatural feel. The sandy area in the square was left for real estate, but the course owner – His Highness Sheikh Mohammed bin Rashid Al Maktoum – has left the area in its natural state.

obstructions. With a piece of land like this you can route the course anywhere you want. This is so much easier than designing in the mountains with trees, rocks, and streams affecting every decision."

What did prove tricky, however, was pinpointing a location in the first place. Several sites were suggested but, each time, local Bedouin tribesmen objected that they lay on camel-grazing routes.

EMIRATES CLUB, MAJLIS COURSE **117**

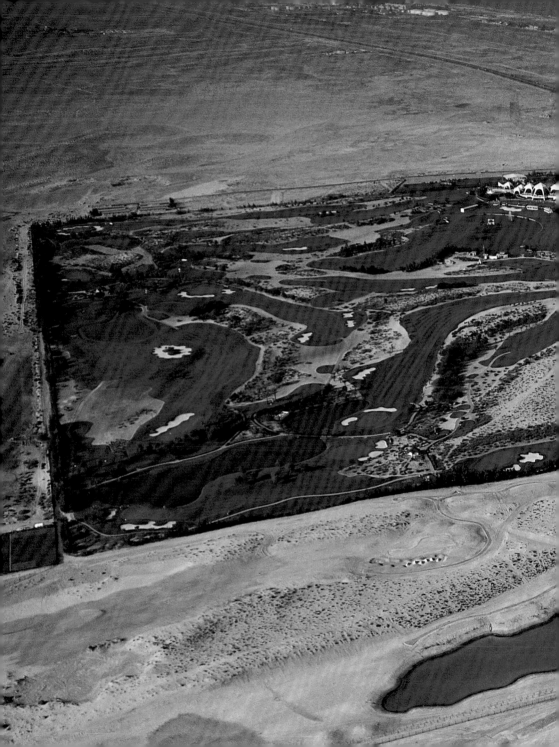

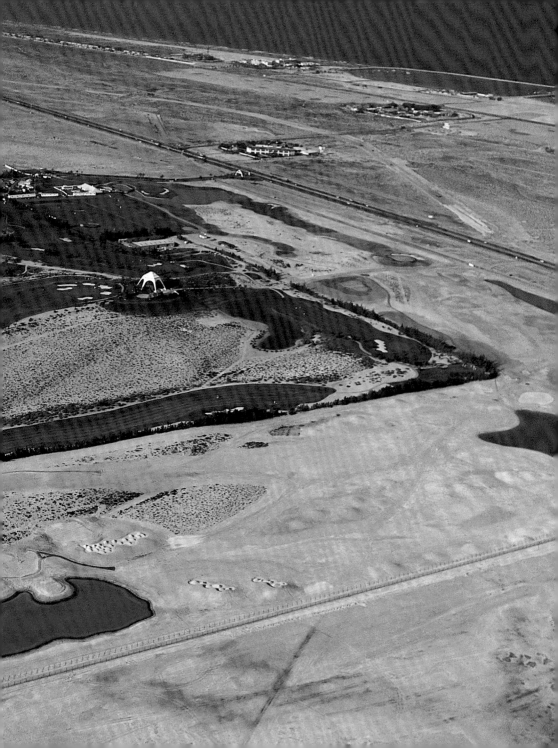

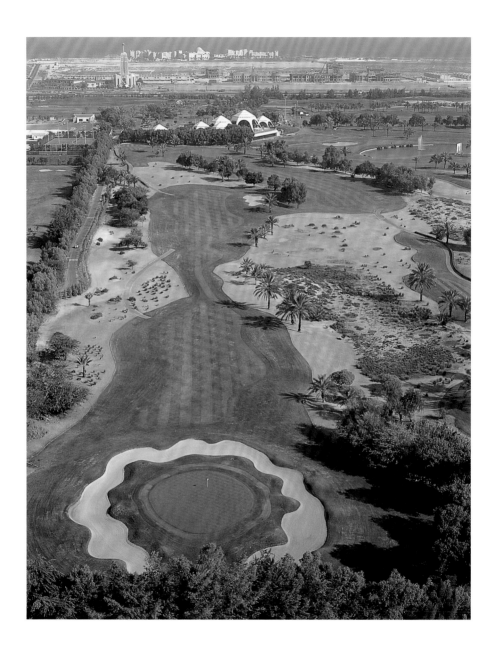

Sensitive to the nomadic Bedouin's needs, Sheikh Mohammed upheld every objection until he was sure the course could be built on spare land.

Litten also encountered problems with the mighty sand dunes that give the course its characteristic changes in elevation. "The trouble with sand dunes is they tend to move about," he recalls. "We would mark out the proposed fairways with 7 foot (2.1m) poles, and come back the next day to find the tops poking out of the sand. We therefore decided to stabilize the dunes by watering them. It worked – not only did it stop the dust flying about, but it also helped the grass to grow. Grass roots go down about 1 foot (0.3m) and that stabilised the dunes even more."

Visitors to the Emirates Club are sometimes perplexed by the rows of 30 foot (9.1m) trees that surround the course and block its views. But this was another crucial tactical move, designed to stop desert winds buzzing the fairways and depositing sand. An everyday sandstorm in the United Arab Emirates can reduce vision to less than 50 feet (15m). The trees also helped to keep out vagrant camels which threatened to chew up the pristine fairways. Today, the golfer's only views of the desert are from the course's elevated spots, most notably the spectacular 8th green.

Before Litten began to irrigate, the area mapped out for the course had just one tree, on what is now the 6th hole. But as he watered, a strange thing happened: "Plants that we didn't know were there

◀ **Desert miracle**
The Majlis Course at Dubai's Emirates Club is the first green course in the Middle East. The course is bordered by 30 foot (9.1m) trees to stop the sands (and wild camels) encroaching onto the pristine fairways. The fabulous par-5 10th – running away from the Bedouin tent-themed clubhouse – sums up the challenge.

started to grow everywhere," he says. "There must have been seeds in the sand, waiting for years to find sufficient water to germinate. Suddenly we had date palm trees, coconut palms, camel grass, petunias, flame trees and more."

Litten flew in Bermuda grass seed from Georgia. It's a grass strain that loves hot weather, thriving at 32°C (90°F) or more. He also added seven lakes, both fresh and salt water, and he and left a 12-acre (4.8 ha) chunk of desert within the course boundary for future development. But Sheikh Mohammed, in keeping with his overall ambition to preserve the desert's natural feel as much as possible, has left those areas vacant.

Litten recalls opening the course to a mixed reception: "The Arabs didn't know what to make of it. I think they were more interested in the birds that had been drawn to the area, and the fish in the lake. But the Europeans loved it. It was accepted as a world-class course from day one."

The Emirates' most memorable holes are the par-5 10th, with a green encircled by sand, and the 8th, which runs uphill to the authentic Bedouin Majlis, or meeting place, that gives the course its name. Its most feared hazard is the thick desert grass that borders the rough. The grass is so wiry that if you fell into it you'd need help to get out.

The first ever grassed golf course in the Middle East, the Majlis proved something of a trend-setter. Abu Dhabi and Bahrain each now have their own grassed courses, and Egypt's course portfolio has grown to 15.

The Majlis has been a regular stager of the European Tour's Dubai Desert Classic, and today it is universally acclaimed as one of the finest courses in the world – not to mention one of the most extraordinary.

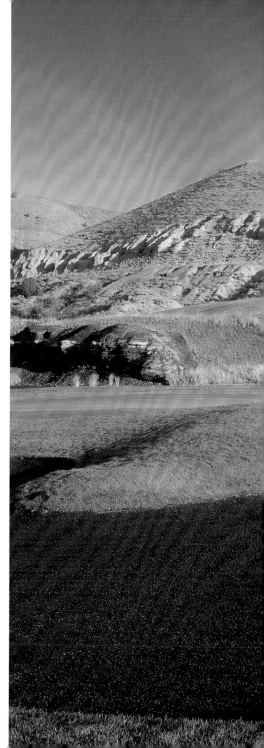

Old Works Golf Course

🍸

SLAG HEAP GOLF

SOMEWHERE BETWEEN THE natural splendour of Montana's Glacier and Yellowstone national parks lies a huge wilderness of black slag. Slag is the by-product of the metal-smelting process, and it is the dominant feature of the old copper-mining town of Anaconda. One slag heap here is so big that if you wanted to load it into boxcars and drive it away, the train would stretch from Seattle to New York. It is hard to imagine more unlikely terrain for a championship 18-holer, yet this is where Old Works Golf Course proudly perches. And it was designed by none other than Jack Nicklaus.

Nicklaus admits that when he first went to work at Anaconda he had no idea what to do with the slag; but once he discovered it was inert and harmless, he decided to integrate it into his design. He exposed huge areas of the material, so that its brilliant blackness would help define the fairways; he sculpted it into landforms, piled it up and built tees on top, and he routed holes through it – notably the spectacular 6th where you must

▶ **Black Bear**
Old Works designer Jack Nicklaus decided to use slag from copper smelting for his bunkers after discovering it was harmless. He tested it himself, building a small trap at a neighbouring course, before giving it the thumbs-up.

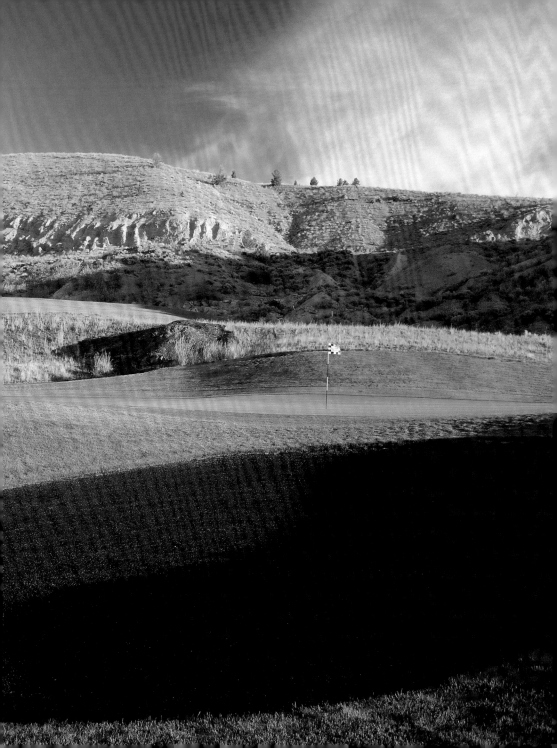

thread your ball between two great heaps of the stuff. It mostly comes into play on the front nine, and dominates three holes.

While working with the slag, Nicklaus picked up a chunk and rubbed it through his fingers. He had a hunch it would make an unusual substitute for bunker sand built a test bunker at a nearby course, filling it with the slag and practising out of it himself. He decided he liked it and, as a result, Old Works has black bunkers. Nicklaus describes it as "a safe, visually stunning way to include the proud history of Anaconda in the golf course."

Old Works course superintendent Rick Hathaway agrees. "Slag is a great bunker material," he says. "It is quite firm, so your ball won't plug in

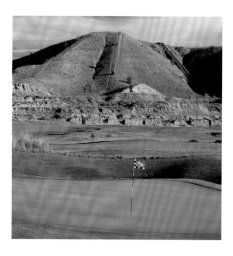

▲ **History lesson**
Copper smelting has not taken place at Anaconda since 1902, but huge hills of the slag by-product still dominate the skyline. Nicklaus even managed to route several holes through the giant mounds. Factory ruins including kilns, furnaces and chimneys are also visible on the hillside.

it. It is grainy and firms up well. It is also angular, so it stays on the bunker slopes instead of slipping to the bottom and forming thick and thin patches. Its firmness means you are best off using a sand-wedge with a flatter sole – not too much bounce. A couple of other clubs have even enquired about using it on their courses."

One other layout that already incorporates slag is The Bear's Best, Las Vegas, a course comprising tributes to Jack Nicklaus's best holes. The course has copied two holes from Old Works – the par-4 2nd and the par-37th – and even went to the trouble of sending a couple of lorries north to Montana to haul down a load of slag.

Old Works stretches to an awesome 7,700 yards (7,041m) off the back tees; but it is a public course and Nicklaus designed it accordingly, with wide approaches to large greens and an emphasis on having fun. He says: "The course offers a challenging and enjoyable experience for the average golfer who plays from the appropriate tees, and thinks his or her way round."

On the face of it, playing through dusky slag hills does not sound very appealing. Yet even with a short season, the course attracts 25,000 visitors a year. Most players say they enjoy the sight of its glossy, cliff-like formations. Also appreciated are the club's efforts to preserve the historic nature of the site. Massive furnace walls line some of the fairways; the huge rock foundations of the smelter border two holes and there are remnants of the flues on the hillsides. There is even talk of installing interpretative plaques.

The staff at Old Works have also had to put a few minds at rest over the cleanliness and healthiness of the site. This area smelted copper from 1884 to 1902, and the mining operation left

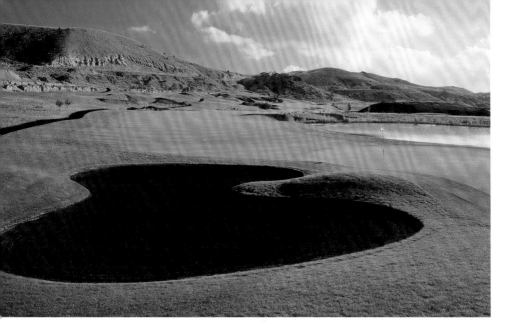

the soil contaminated with concentrations of arsenic, lead and copper. Scattered throughout were piles of rubble and garbage. Before Nicklaus could start work on the course, the entire area had to be "capped", adding a layer of clean material to the soiled land surface. The cap took a year to apply, and has three layers of limerock to counteract the waste soil's acidity; 15 inches (381mm) of clay soil to prevent water washing down through the contaminated earth and polluting the aquifer below; and finally a layer of sandy soil to promote growth. The total thickness of the cap is 2 feet (0.6m).

"The bedrock of the entire project was public safety," says Rick Hathaway. We had the Environmental Protection Agency here every day, making sure there was no problem. There is no stench, or anything like that."

The idea of building the course on this peculiar patch of land came not from Nicklaus but from the people of Anaconda. After it closed down, the Old Works site was left to fester until 1983, when the US government drew up a list of ruined waste sites, known as "Superfunds", and earmarked them for clean-up and redevelopment. The Old Works was included. The Atlantic Richfield Company (ARCO), which owned the land, didn't know what to do with it, and gave the people of Anaconda a chance to decide. The response – "build a golf course" – surprised them, but the more they thought about it, the more they liked it.

"The course has a definite museum-like quality," says Hathaway, "but the main feeling you get is of amazement that an area of wasteland could be turned into such a great test of golf."

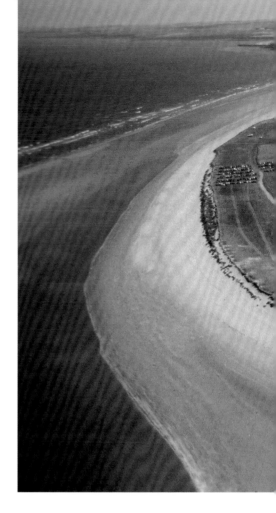

St Andrews, Old Course

QUIRKY HOLES DESIGNED BY TIME

THE OLD COURSE AT St Andrews is regarded as the oldest course in the world, and it is certainly one of the weirdest. It can be played backwards as well as forwards. It features seven enormous double greens – the 5th/13th spreads across 50,000 square feet (4,645sqm). Surprise pot bunkers festoon the fairways which are so hard to spot that an emergency vehicle once sped straight into one. The fairways run across a maze of forgotten roads, and are riddled with crazy humps that specialize in kicking a straight shot sideways into the bushes. And, on the 17th, you must drive the ball over some abandoned railway sheds. "Say, that looks like some deserted old course over there," said the American legend Sam Snead on his first visit. "I wonder what they called it?"

Perhaps the principal challenge for golfers is coming to terms with the severe swings in fortune that these disorienting hazards inflict. On his first trip to the Old Course in 1921, the great American Bobby Jones tore up his scorecard in fury after getting stuck in a deep bunker, but in 1929 he made a glorious return, winning the Open Championship. "At no place but St Andrews would these hazards

be acceptable," he said later, "but on the Old Course they are as natural as the grey stone of the houses which line the closing hole."

The Old Course is so eccentric because it was built on common land. King David I of Scotland gave the land to the people in 1123, telling them they could do what they pleased on it, for free. In the 600-year history of golf at St Andrews, golfers have had to play past people using the course for

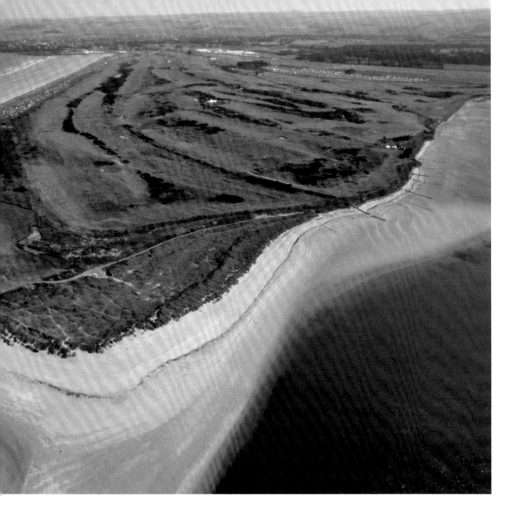

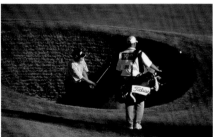

▲ Public spirit

The Old Course of St Andrews sits on common land given to the people in the twelfth century. Apart from golf, the terrain has also been used for sheep grazing, horse riding, archery, football and, in many cases, dog walking.

◀ Hidden bunkers

Deep, hard-to-spot bunkers are scattered indiscriminately around the course, with no particular rhyme or reason. The great American Bobby Jones had to bow out of his first game on the course in 1921, after getting stuck in one.

> ## "An early round here would have been more like a hike than the game we know today."

▼

PETER MASON

rabbit breeding, sheep grazing, cloth bleaching, rifle shooting, horse riding, archery and football.

The course is still subject to ancient common laws. The womenfolk of St Andrews are perfectly entitled to wash their clothes in the famous Swilcan Burn that crosses the 1st and 18th holes, though they must be careful not to violate a by-law that forbids you to stir up the silt at the bottom. Nor is there anything to stop them drying those clothes by spreading them on the nearby gorse bushes.

What's more, until 1993 a law allowed the Laird of the Strathtyrum Estate to dig up shells on the course any time he pleased. He had not exercised that right since 1955.

The unorthodox status of the land goes some way to explaining the weird undulations of the St Andrews links. It was once common practice for the townsfolk to dig out turf from the course to roof their houses, and this carried on into the early nineteenth century. This habit may have been terrific for home insulation but it left the fairways pitted and pock-marked. Similarly, most of the paths and roads around the town were surfaced with shells and, again, the best source

▼ Six feet under

"Hell bunker", on the 14th, is the largest trap on the Old Course. Shortly after this you must avoid "Grave bunker". You come to "Hell" before the "Grave" because the course was being played in the reverse direction when they were named.

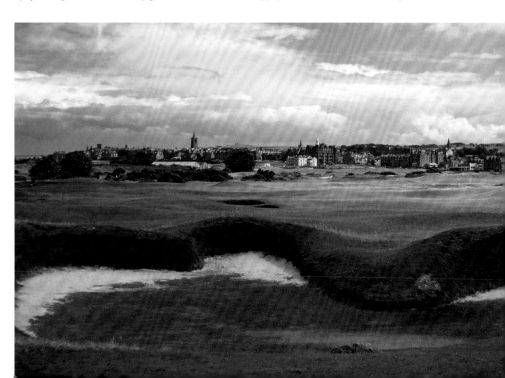

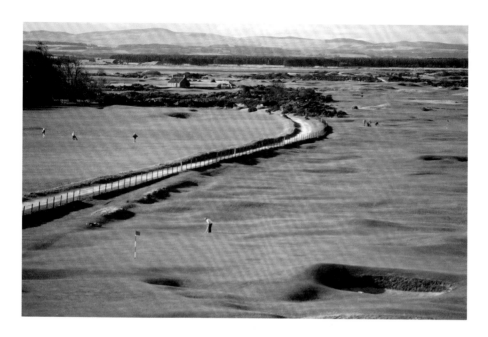

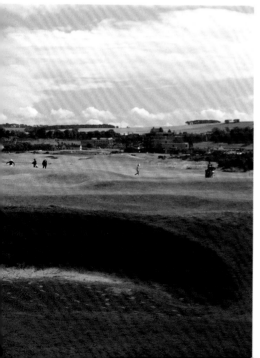

▲ **Rough with the smooth**

The ground of the Old Course is heavily pitted. One American professional once said that the course needed a good clean and press. The age-old traditions of digging for shells on the course, as well as digging up turf for roof insulation, have not helped form a smooth playing surface.

for these was the golf course. This meant yet more excavating and more exposed hollows, some of which may ultimately have become the first bunkers. Over time, other bunkers were formed by the enlargement of rabbit holes, or by dunes collapsing.

"An early round here would have been more like a hike than the game we know today," says Peter Mason of the St Andrews Links Trust. "The 6th hole is called 'Heathery', because its original green was a mixture of heather and shells."

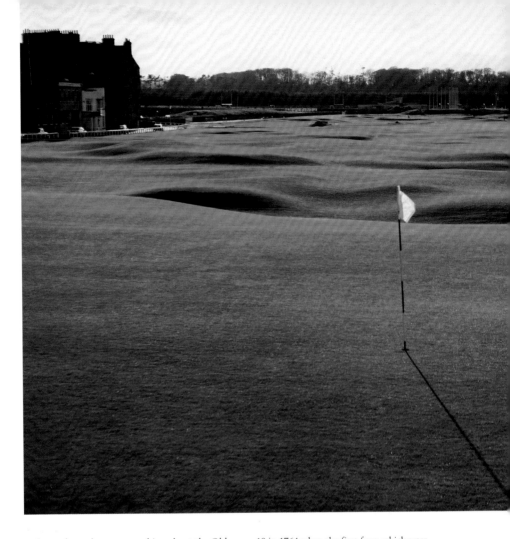

But perhaps the strangest thing about the Old Course remains its double greens, which allow it to be tackled backwards as well as forwards. Indeed, the way the links is played today – anti-clockwise from the clubhouse – is the reverse of what was originally intended.

The course began with 22 holes, and golfers played out and back to the same flags. This became

18 in 1764 when the first four, which were considered too short, were combined into two longer holes. Golfers were happy with the nine-out, nine-back format until 1848 when the cheap "gutta percha" golf ball replaced the pricy "feathery". Hordes took up the game, and suddenly the course became congested. The practice of groups hitting to the same hole from opposite directions became

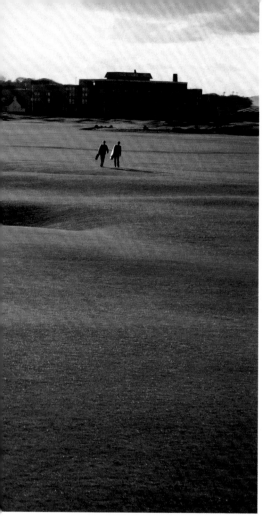

◀ Coming home

The 18th hole at St Andrews is a short flat par-4. Virtually featureless and very flat, it is a curiously bland finale to a singular round of golf. The depression in front of the green, known as the "Valley of Sin", was once much deeper but has softened over the years. The paucity of features on the hole is more than compensated for by the thrill of playing back into the town on the oldest fairway in the world.

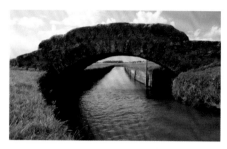

▲ Stone-washed

The famous stone Swilcan bridge spans the famous burn which crosses the 1st and 18th fairways. It was not built for golfers but to take people from the town to the old harbour in the Eden estuary. An ancient byelaw allows St Andrews denizens to wash their clothes in the water.

tiresome, not to mention dangerous. So a second hole was installed in each green. The course widened naturally to accommodate approaches to both pins from opposing directions.

When these two-flag greens were first introduced, the course was played clockwise. The first hole took golfers from near the present 1st tee to the present 17th green. They then played from what is now the 18th tee to the 16th green, and so on, which explains why the bunkering is so random today, especially on the current back nine. Many troubled golfers play the course in reverse.

St Andrews is peculiar because it was designed by time, not by man. The first deliberate human influence came in 1864, by which time the links had had 450 years to evolve. Even then the changes were minimal – the great Old Tom Morris widened the course, modified the 18th green and built a new 1st green, allowing St Andrews to be played in reverse. For a while, play alternated between clockwise one week and anti-clockwise the next, but the new anti-clockwise direction became more popular. It remains the favoured direction today.

Stone Canyon Club

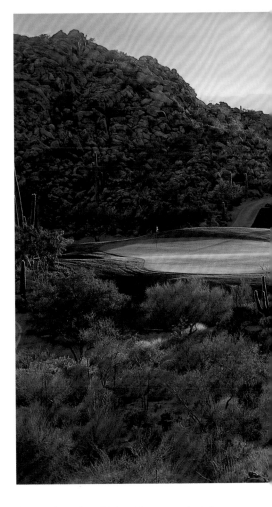

DESERT GOLF THAT
BITES BACK

STONE CANYON CLUB, to the south of Tucson, takes you deep into the arid wilderness of the Sonoran desert. Its holes traverse rocky terrain, running through natural arroyos and gulleys. It would look like a moonscape were it not for the enormous Saguaro cacti, which dwarf humans and can live for up to 300 years. The course's island fairways, shards of jade lacerating the rock-strewn landscape, are as immaculate as they are elusive. Several holes feature petroglyphs – depictions of snakes, cows and mules drawn on the rocks by the native Hohokam Indians, dating back to 800AD.

The course typifies the American desert layout – spectacular, exciting, penal and, if you stray from the fairways, dangerous. If your ball does err from the lush sanctuary of the fairway, think twice before venturing into the desert to retrieve it. Lurking behind the boulders and those fantastic cacti are gila monsters, mountain lions, bobcats and javelinas (wild boars), not to mention two kinds of deadly rattlesnake, the western diamondback and the green mojave. These slithering terrors often sun themselves on the buggy paths. One golfer tried to run over one, only to find his buggy-wheels flipped it into the air and

deposited it right in his lap. The accepted wisdom about rattlesnakes is that they are scared of people and will not attack unless threatened. There is, however, limited information on what a rattler regards as threatening. Watch out for insecure ones who sense danger at 60 paces.

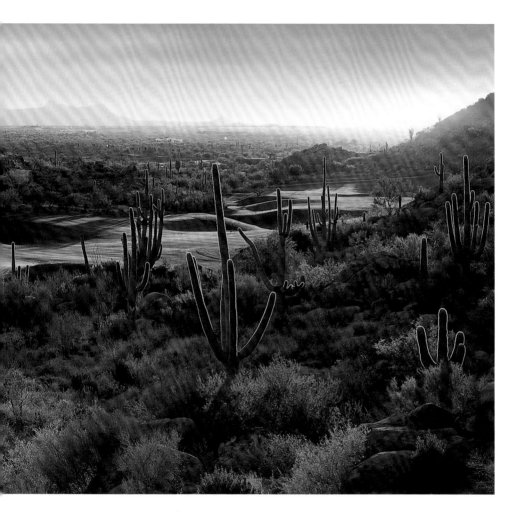

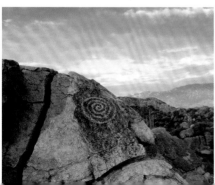

◀▲ **Rocky horror show**

A typically intimidating scene at Stone Canyon Club where craggy desert makes only a token effort to give way to grass. Until the fifteenth century the land was populated by Hohokam Indians who left many rock drawings behind; you can still see some on the ancient rock cluster on the practice ground. This spiral shape represents the sun.

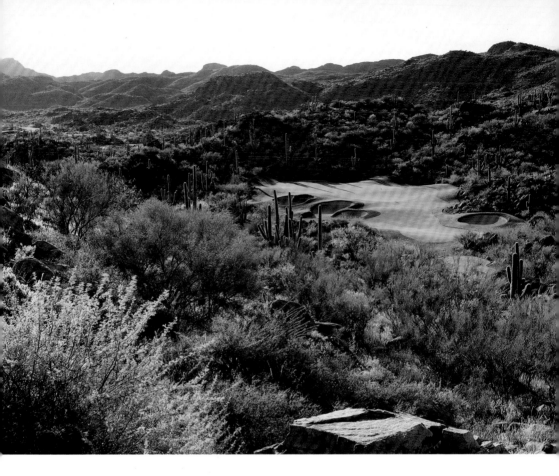

"We have members of staff who are trained to capture and relocate the rattlesnakes," says Stone Canyon's director of golf, Todd Huizinga. "The trouble is, the snakes have in-built homing devices and always come back again. We don't have anyone trained to deal with snake bites, but there are two local fire stations that respond within minutes."

It's not just the wildlife that bites back here: the desert is full of treacherous vegetation. The thorns on a prickly pear are so sharp that they can pierce the soles of your shoes. More worrisome still is the

"We have members of staff who are trained to capture and relocate the rattlesnakes. The trouble is, the snakes have built-in homing devices and always come back again."

Todd Huizinga

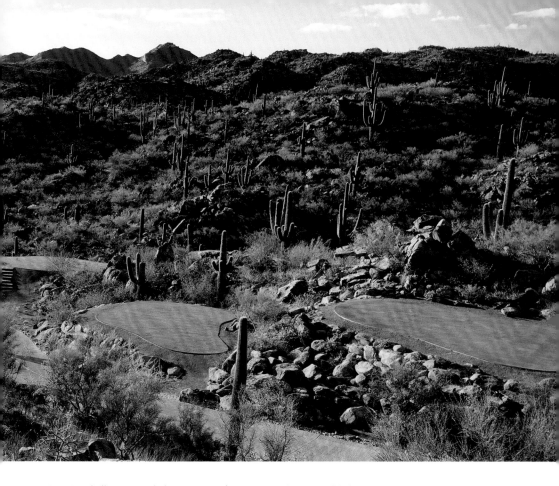

jumping cholla, a particularly spiny type of cactus. Its barbed spines detach so easily that they are said to jump out as you walk past. The South African star Ernie Els fell foul of the jumping cholla at the Andersen Consulting World Championship of Golf, at Scottsdale in 1998, when a spine got stuck in the middle finger of his left hand. A medical crew had to remove three needles from his finger.

Like most desert courses, Stone Canyon has what's known as "limited turf options". In other words, water is scarce and grassed areas must be

▲ **Beauty and the beasts**

The desert surrounding the course is beautifully rugged but if your ball ends up in there it's best to move on. The terrain is the natural habitat of scorpions, rattlesnakes, tarantulas and mountain lions. Most plants are heavily barbed and do not take kindly to golfers trying to build a stance and swing.

kept to a minimum. That means island tees, fairways and greens – and sensational contrasts between these pristine green oases and the surrounding jagged wasteland. The designer, Jay Morrish, is a recognised desert course expert. On a site totalling 1,400 acres (567ha) he has grassed just 90 – and 12 acres (4.9ha) of that are for the practice facilities. Morrish has mastered the art of allocating turf solely to areas that really need it. Working within the turfing restrictions, he has created fairways that stretch 50-70 yards (46-64m) across – but only in the prime driving positions.

"Stone Canyon places a premium on accuracy off the tee," says Todd Huizinga. "With most courses, if you miss a fairway you are simply in the rough or trees. You still have an opportunity to advance your ball. But if you miss the fairway here it can be like hitting into a hazard or going out of bounds. It's hard to play the ball, or even find it."

It really pays to tune up your driving before

▼ **Phallic Classic**
The giant Saguaro cacti which flank the fairways at Stone Canyon can live for up to 300 years. Most clubs have their share of prickly members, but Stone Canyon has more than most.

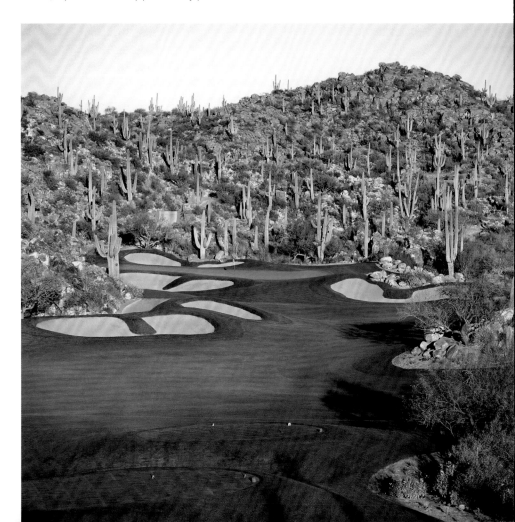

playing in the desert. It's also best to swallow your pride and play from tees that offer you the best chance of hitting the fairway. But knowing the trauma that awaits, should you miss, only adds to the thrill of playing here. Golf's unwritten law states that the more severe the hazard, the greater the pleasure derived from avoiding it. For the best experience here, try evening golf. The crystal-clear desert air is reckoned to produce the most beautiful sunsets in the world.

▶ **Geological extravaganza** (OVERLEAF)

As well as the exciting rocky terrain, designer Jay Morrish also had the spectacular Santa Catalina mountains to help make Stone Canyon special. Peaking at nearly 10,000 feet (3,048m), the mountains add tremendously to this playing experience – your flying ball is constantly framed against them.

▼ **Sward of destiny**

Stone Canyon's landing areas are not ungenerous, but if you miss them it's a lost ball. Morrish was careful to build the course with minimum disruption to the natural terrain – cacti, desert lavendar and jumping cholla will all hide your ball.

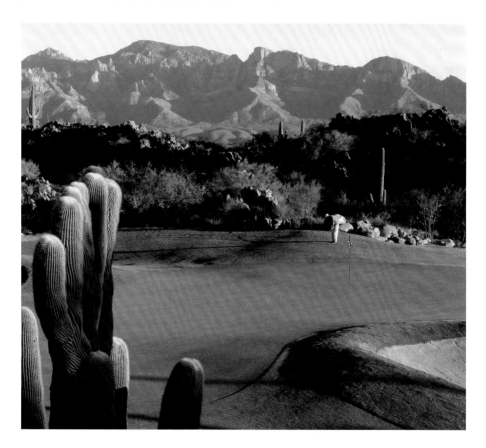

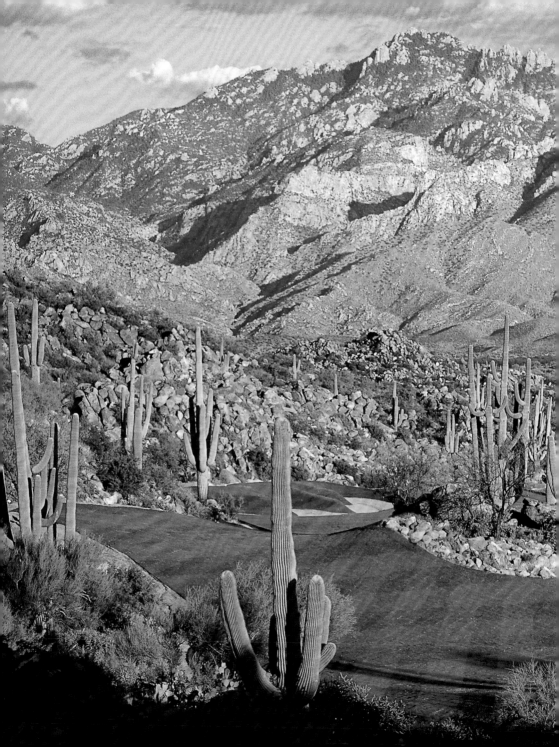

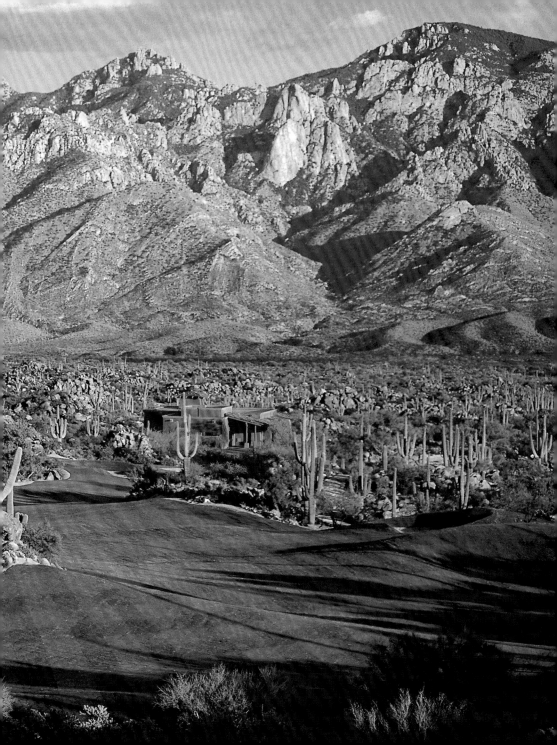

Macon la Salle Golf Club

♟

EROTIC GOLF

NESTLING AMONG THE JUICY vines of Burgundy is the world's first and only erotic golf course. Viewed from the air, the holes of Macon la Salle, laid out in 1987, portray a writhing mass of female bodies in assorted compromising positions. Perhaps the course's signature hole is the par-5 11th, a dogleg featuring the silhouette of a naked woman on a chair. Golfers attempting to cut the corner face the unlikely prospect of getting their ball stuck in her vagina, represented by a gaping triangular bunker. In addition, two heaving, breastlike mounds wait to kick a slovenly approach into the rough 80 yards (73m) short of the green, which represents her head.

Each hole is reckoned to teach you a lesson about golf and women. The 6th drums into you the need for length, while the 9th preaches the need for application and concentration. The members describe the course as behaving exactly like a woman. "Sometimes she is meek and submissive, and presents herself for your enjoyment," says Florian Treves. "At others she will grab your balls if you don't pay her enough attention!"

Macon la Salle's holes may resemble body parts, but their anatomy is not immediately apparent to the golfer. The design works on the same principle as the ancient Nazca Lines of Peru – confusing at ground level, but get up high and dazzling shapes emerge. The 10th hole is a great example. The tee seems fairly unremarkable but is, in fact, located in the navel of a reclining mademoiselle. The hole leads you past voluptuous hips and down a sinuous leg to reach the green – which is, of course, shaped like a foot.

"It is hard to understand while you are playing," says course manager Francois Terard. "The design is difficult to see. It is only really evident on the 11th, where you can see the two mounds in front of the green."

The man responsible is course architect Robert Berthet. "Too often golfers are interested only in their own score," he sighs. "My hope is to make players realize that a golf course is not just a golf course, it is also a landscape, a piece of land with a history. Burgundy is a country of pleasure, of sensuality. I couldn't have built this just anywhere."

Berthet believes passionately that golf courses risk being monotonous unless they have a unique theme. His current project, a course near Dunkirk,

> "My hope is to make players realize that a golf course is not just a golf course, it is also a landscape, a piece of land with a history."
>
> ♟
>
> ROBERT BERTHET

▶ **Ogling from aloft**
The sensuous shapes of designer Robert Berthet's holes are not always obvious to golfers playing on the ground. Once up in the air, however, the shape of their anatomy becomes much more apparent.

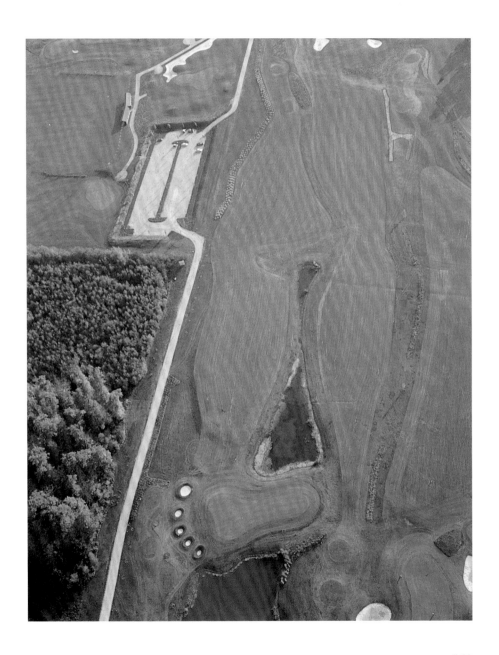

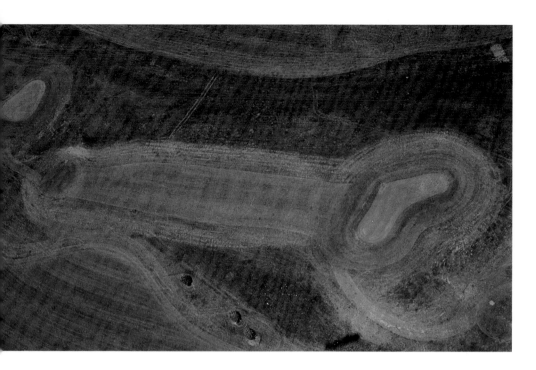

▲ **Stiff test**

Course director Patrick de la Chesnais felt obliged to add a couple of "male" holes to Macon de la Salle after the original layout, an erotic homage to the female form, was branded chauvinistic and sexist.

which is designed on the principles of a seventeenth-century fortification laid out by Vauban, King Louis XIV's military engineer. "I want my courses to make golfers more poetic," he says.

Berthet chose the female form over the male because he felt that smooth, feminine curves and contours would be more in harmony with a golfing landscape. His own favourite hole is the 14th: "This is a womanleg, as opposed to a dogleg. I couldn't have designed this course without a very special lady to inspire me. I had a muse in mind when I designed the course – she's called Nicole – and the leg is a perfect representation of hers."

The course was opened in 1990 by the British Ryder Cup player Paul Way – and immediately

provoked accusations of sexism. As a response, former course director Patrick de la Chesnais saw to it that a "male" hole, ramrod straight, was added to Macon's sister course, a nine-holer. This is a 180-yard (165m) par-3, but for some reason the club's male members tend to exaggerate its length.

"The male hole is not really that apparent anymore," smiles Francois Terard. "Or at least, it really depends on how we mow the grass."

Despite his homage to the female form, Berthet

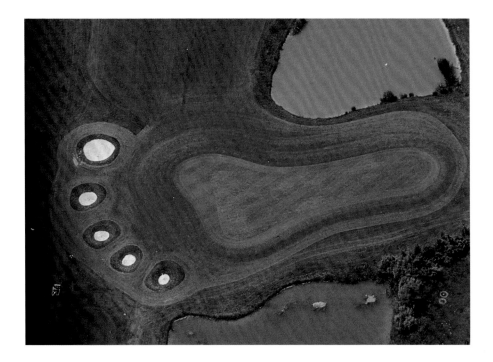

▲ Toe's the line

Designer Robert Berthet has managed to represent every part of the female form within Macon's 18 holes, down to the little toe on the distinctive 10th green. Berthet's muse was a mademoiselle named Nicole.

believes he has not compromised the status of Macon la Salle as a serious test of golf. "Look at any course from the air and it is very easy to compare the proportions of a golf hole to a human body," he argues. "On a standard course, an average hole is 383 yards (350m) long and 16 yards (15m) wide. Since those proportions are easily found on the human body it is quite simple to make the adaptation. The green is like a face, when you look at sizes and contours."

The designer points out that man has always depicted large-scale figures of humans and animals in the landscape. "There are a great number of huge, white chalk horses in England, and there is the Long Man of Cerne Abbas too. The Nazca Lines do the same thing, and even at St Andrews in Scotland there are bunkers called the 'Lion's Mouth' and the 'Principal's Nose'."

De la Chesnais, the man who asked Berthet to design this course, is delighted with the result. "We wanted something esoteric and typically French. Something artistic and memorable. We didn't want another American-style course. I think we've succeeded – what could be more memorable than playing golf over a lot of nude ladies?"

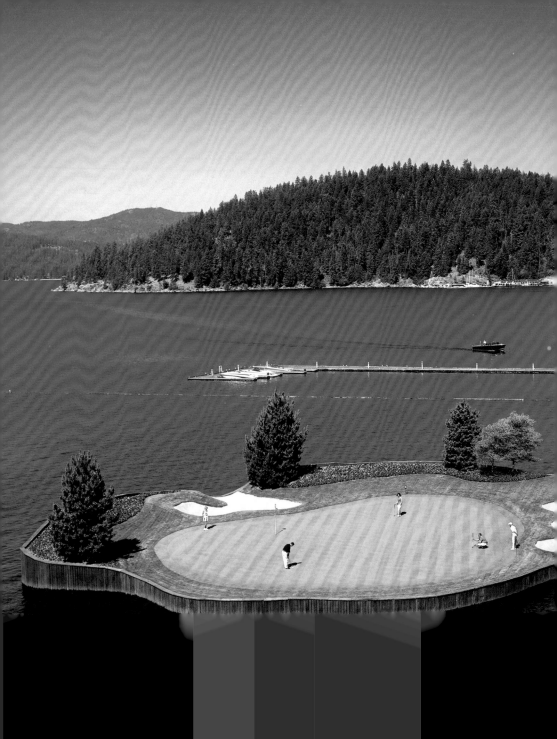

Coeur d'Alene Resort

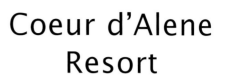

14TH, 150-220 YARDS (137-201M) – HITTING TO A FLOATING GREEN

THE STAFF AT COEUR D'ALENE report an average of five holes-in-one per year on their floating-green 14th. If a hole-in-one on a floating green seems impossible to you, be assured that the putting surface is not actually bobbing around. Constructed on a honeycomb of concrete cells filled with Styrofoam, the green is anchored to a cable so that it can be pulled back and forth. Every night the course superintendent does just that, setting and anchoring a new challenge for the following day. The green weighs 5 million pounds (2.27million kilos) and does not bob up and down, even in strong winds. Players report it to be every bit as stable as the other 17 on this impeccably manicured resort course.

Thanks to its moving target, the 14th can play anything between 150 and 220 yards (137-201m) from the same tee. Also, the hole is in something of a goldfish bowl. It can be seen from most points on

◀ **Hope floats**

The floating green is a homage to Coeur d'Alene's lumber history, when stacks of bundled-up logs were frequently seen drifting down the lake. It is moved back and forth by cables, and a forecaddie gives you your yardage for the day.

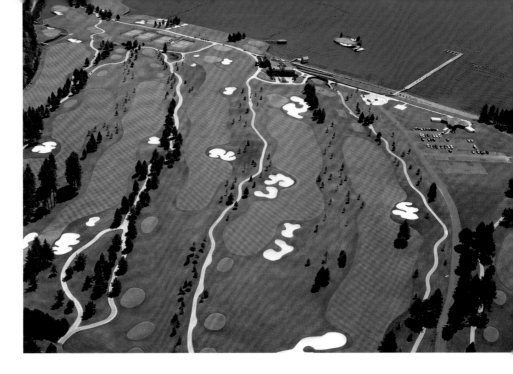

the course, and from the nearby snack bar where sadists have an unfortunate habit of gathering. Unsure of the yardage and which club to use, the golfer must rely on his forecaddie. At Coeur d'Alene Resort, every group is assigned one for the day. He does everything for you, from cleaning your clubs to ordering your lunch, but at the 14th his job is yardage. He fires a laser at a reflector positioned on the flag, and is able to give his group an accurate distance figure. It ought to help, but somehow this hi-tech precision only adds to the pressure of the shot.

In order to keep play moving, the club has passed a rule allowing a maximum of two tee shots per player. If you fail with both you must advance to the green (on a small mahogany vessel named the "Putting Boat") and take a drop. The boat runs along a second cable. It seems that people are

pretty good at obeying the two-shot rule because Coeur d'Alene's diver reports scooping out 40,000 balls from 30,000 rounds played.

"We get some people who don't like it, though," grins pro Mark Nelson. "They are going to stay there till they hit the green. But we have to enforce the rule to stop the course snarling up. The 14th takes 20 minutes to play as it is."

Some people who have played the hole badly suggest it would be more fun if you could tee off while it was moving. "That's never been tried," shrugs Nelson. "The hole is not a gimmick. I think it's fine as it is. All people remember is whether

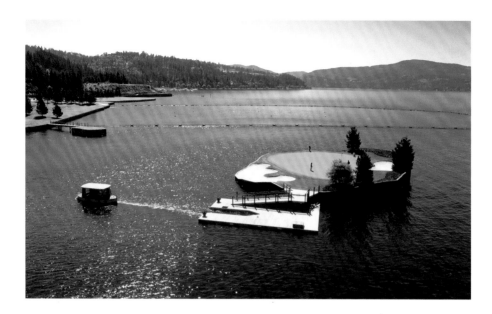

▲ **Lady of the lake**

Golfers reach the green via a small vessel affectionately known as the "Putting Boat". Attached to another cable, she takes her time ferrying golfers back and forth to the green, and the hole takes 20 minutes to complete.

they hit the floating green. And they like to joke that all putts break towards the water."

Although architect Scott Miller designed the 14th, the concept came from owner Duane Hagadone, builder of the first resort here in the mid-1980s. Hagadone fondly recalled the days when Coeur d'Alene was one of north-west America's largest lumber centres, and huge clusters of logs were often seen gliding on the lake. He saw a floating green as the perfect way to remind golfers and resort guests of the area's heritage.

The floating hole is set against a stunning backdrop. Coeur d'Alene Lake has 135 miles (217km) of gorgeous shoreline, with tranquil coves, tree-lined shores and sandy beaches. Ospreys plunge into the lake almost as often as golf balls, and at night its mirror-like surface coruscates with the lights from the resort and downtown Coeur d'Alene. It was voted one of America's most pristine lakes by *National Geographic* magazine. It is also where the first ever water skis were tried out, by John Finney in the 1920s.

Five holes-in-one per year is one for every 6,000 rounds played. Slim odds, but if you get one you will get the red carpet treatment – literally. "When someone makes an ace we roll out a red carpet in front of the pro shop," says Mark Nelson. "Everyone in the shop applauds as you walk up. We hand you a hole-in-one trophy with the details of your shot: date, yardage and so on. It is a great memento of a special shot on a special hole."

Extreme Secrets

Y

UNSUNG COURSES THAT
SERVE UP BIZARRE GOLF

EXTREME DESIGN

The Machrie Hotel

ISLAY, SCOTLAND – BLIND
GUESSWORK IN THE DUNES

THE MODERN-DAY MANIA for logic and fairness in golf design has homogenised the typical golf course challenge. Fairways must be the proper width for the hole, greens the correct size for the length of approach. Fairway slopes must be levelled and hazards must be seen. The course's test becomes predictable and boring, making players cry out for a challenge which offers something different.

The Machrie Hotel, on the island of Islay off the west coast of Scotland, is the perfect antidote. This time-warp of a golf course is as curious as they come. Instead of running alongside the dunes like most Scottish links courses, its holes tackle them head on, running up and over. The result is a series of extraordinary blind holes. Your usual downhole view of a flat fairway and distant green is replaced by a huge hillock rising up in front of you, often with a marker post on the top.

The blindness marks its zenith on the 400-yard (366m) 7th. A vast dune blocks your sight of the fairway. It's so intimidating that some of the older members have asked the greenkeeper to mow a bail-out area to the side to help them play around. Even if you manage to clear the dune with your tee shot, you'll find another knoll blocking your approach to the green. Only a marker post behind the green gives you a rough idea where you should be heading.

Islay is famous for its whisky and has seven working distilleries. The locals will tell you that the course makes a lot more sense once you've knocked back a tot or two. The visiting golfer's pre-shot routine becomes a festival of head-scratching and shoulder shrugging. There is nothing else to do but make a guess at where the fairway might be, offer up a prayer to the god of golf and blast over the hill with equal measures of hope and desperation.

With such a blind course, you may think local knowledge would be invaluable. But the course has so many natural intricacies that nobody can ever say they really know how to play it. "I don't think anyone can truly say they know it all," says one. "I will never, ever get tired of trying to work it out, and I can't think of too many other courses, even links, that I can say that about."

While today's golfers might curse and swear at the apparent injustice of not being able to see their target, the players of yesteryear loved it. In the late nineteenth century, the gentlemen of the day liked their game of golf to mirror their lives – full of unexpected challenges and annoyances. So when designer Willie Campbell built the course in 1891, he saw the mighty dunes as perfectly irrational obstacles for the golfer to negotiate, rather than unreasonable hills to be levelled in the name of logic.

Despite the addition of five modern holes to the course in the Seventies, this blind course stands as a relic to the ultra-natural course designs of the nineteenth century. We are lucky it still exists, as the advent of the bulldozer and the new appetite for fairness meant the hills of many blind holes were flattened.

The Machrie's head greenkeeper, Simon Freeman, believes he knows why the Machrie escaped the diggers: "The Machrie retains its blindness to the extent that it is now a freak, and I think that is purely because it is on an island. The golfers who played the Machrie in the Twenties and Thirties – when other blind hills on the mainland were being bulldozed – simply didn't know any different. That is why they never complained."

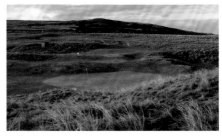

▲ *At Machrie Hotel golfers must blast over the dunes blind, with no idea where they should be aiming.*

The Elfego Baca Shoot

NEW MEXICO, USA – LONG DISTANCE GOLF

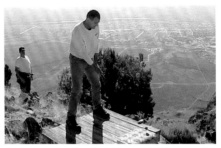

▲ *6am tee time at the top of the mountain. From here this golfer must descend 2,500 feet (762m) to reach his target.*

NEW MEXICO IS THE UFO capital of the world, and every June strange orbs are spotted in the skies over Socorro Peak, south of Albuquerque. Unfortunately for Ufologists, the only ETs around here are Extreme Terrain golfers and the mysterious orbs nothing more than gaudy golf balls. Socorro Peak is the venue for the annual Elfego Baca Shoot, a surreal golfing event played over just one hole. But what a hole. It is 2.5 miles (4km) long, and runs down the side of a mountain.

This bizzare tournament is limited to ten golfers. At dawn they are ferried up to the top of Socorro Peak in four-wheel-drive wagons for a 6am tee off. From here they must slog their way down the mountain to a distant 50-foot (15.2m) diameter circle, known as "The Hole", 2,550 feet (762m) below them at 4,730ft (1,442m). In their way to scupper them is a near vertical fairway teeming with scorpions, canyons, disused mine shafts, rocks, rattlesnakes, vicious cacti and voracious black gnats.

Each competitor plays down the mountain in a one-ball. He or she is allowed to bring up to three ball-spotters, and is accompanied by a safety expert who doubles as a scorer. Your final score is made up of the total number of shots it has taken you to manoeuvre your ball into the circle, plus the number of balls you have lost. The winner has the lowest total.

The undisputed king of long-distance mountain golf is 6-handicapper Mike Stanley. He has won the event 18 of the 19 times he has played in it, usually with a score in the mid teens. He carries just a driver and 5-iron, but only uses the latter for the last, precision shots into the circle. "The key to my success is my spotters," he declares nobly. "I have people who are really good at finding my ball. They'll pile headlong into cacti, bush scrub, in fact almost anything, to find it. My tactics are to send my spotters down the mountain to where I think I might hit the ball, and then I try to hit them with the ball – which I have never managed to do."

The most exhilarating part of the contest has to be the first tee shot. Your teeing ground is a small rectangular wooden box, wedged crudely into the mountainside. Stand on the tee and you will find it takes all of your concentration to look away from the astonishing view over New Mexico and down at your ball. If the morning is clear you can see for 100 miles (161km) up and down the Rio Grande valley. Tumbling away below you is the Socorro mountain. The freedom, adrenalin, thin air and view downhill conspire to give you a mighty start.

Your journey down the mountainside is aided by several rules. You are allowed to place your ball on a piece of carpet which becomes your golf course; you can move your ball 50 feet (15m) from its lie but no nearer to the hole; lose a ball and you will receive a one-shot penalty but no loss of distance, and you are given 20 minutes to find your ball instead of the usual five.

Dennis Hunter, the man responsible for the safety of the 50 or so on the mountain, knows all about the hazards. "It's very steep with lots of slippery rocks," he warns. "My major concern is people falling down and breaking arms and legs. Usually in the morning we'll see rattlesnakes. Black gnats are everywhere and can give you a hell of a nip. They particularly like to get in your ears and hair. We therefore recommend hats, long-sleeved shirts and long trousers – and of course bug spray."

One of event's most common accidents is people slipping and falling into the ubiquitous prickly pear and cholla cacti. "I've done it and it's no fun," says Stanley. "You can expect to find a dozen sharp needles in you; tweezers are an essential part of your kit. Once I was being followed by two reporters from the *El Paso Times*. One slipped and fell in the cactus. I'll always remember the sight of the guy with his pants around his ankles while his buddy pulled needles out of his backside."

Given all the hardship, one may wonder what on earth incites Stanley to come back year after year. "I often wonder that myself," he laughs.

The Himalayan Club

POKHARA, NEPAL – THE WORLD'S MOST HIDDEN COURSE

THE SMALL HIMALAYAN TOWN of Pokhara is set in the foothills of the Annapurnas, a range that boasts the world's 10th highest mountain and seven peaks of over 23,000 feet (7,010m). It lies 200 miles (322km) west of Everest and 100 miles (161km) west of the Nepali capital, Kathmandu. It is beside a lake, and makes an ideal base camp for trekking among the foothills. But this unlikely setting is also a great spot for golf. Pokhara can justly claim to have one of the world's most remarkable golf courses – the Himalayan Club.

The nine-hole course measures just 3,360 yards (3,072m), but extreme elevation changes mean that a round here takes more than three hours. The clubhouse and the first three holes are set up on a plateau, but the 4th – a 495-yard (453m) par-5 known as "Leopard's Lair" – sweeps you down into an abyss. The fast-flowing Bijaypur river has carved out a gigantic chasm in the plateau, and for the next few holes you play alongside, over and between channels of rushing water.

The course meanders on through this spellbinding amphitheatre, and your route to the green of the only par-3, the 8th, takes you across a fearfully frail, water-battered bridge. The hole is called "Bluepool Rock". The 9th green is also at the bottom of the canyon, leaving you with a lung-busting trek up the ravine, via a narrow goat track, to the clubhouse. Mercifully, it offers ample relaxion and a huge verandah, and resembles an Indian tea plantation bungalow. All this is set against the crystalline backdrop of the Annapurnas, about 20 miles (32km) away. At dawn the mountains are most spectacular when they take on a mesmerising pink hue.

This remote golf course does not see many visitors, but those who do come invariably file thrilling reports. "The first thing that hits you is total amazement that anyone would actually build a golf course there," says Englishman John Minney. "The second is how much fun the course is going to be to play because of its unusual terrain".

But Minney did not bargain for the difficulty of getting there. The one and only route to the course takes about half an hour on the dustiest, ruttiest track imaginable, heavily pitted by dried-up streams. He took a 4X4, but

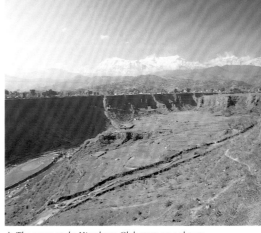

▲ *The course at the Himalayan Club starts on a plateau, but soon plunges down into an abyss by the Bijaypur river.*

even then actually had to get out and push it a couple of times. The visitor's best plan is to stay at the nearby Pokhara Lodge Hotel, which arranges golf at the course for its guests.

Once arrived, golfers must also get used to some unusual playing conditions. The grass is thick, wiry and brown. Your ball perches on top of it – although there is a decent layer of earth underneath to enable you to take a divot. The greens are in reasonable condition though.

The course was designed and built by an ex-British Army officer, Major Ram Gurung MBE. It took him three years to create the holes out of wasteland, river and rocks. "I wanted to preserve the natural environment so that you can experience the beautiful Nepali scenery while playing a challenging round of golf," Gurung says.

The feeling of being at one with nature is intensified by the flora and fauna of the Himalayan Club. Wild geraniums spring up all over the course, and you've a chance of spotting foxes, monkeys, hawks and eagles during your round. The monkeys will not approach you – you can get within 30 yards (27m) before they run away. They will not make off with your ball, although you may worry about hitting them. The presence of leopards and tigers add to the excitement, but in fact they are very rarely seen.

Despite its mountain location, the Himalayan Club enjoys a subtropical climate. Summer days average a pleasant 27˚C (81˚F), while winter temperatures hover around 12˚C (54˚F). The elevation means it never gets uncomfortably hot although, as you slog up that goat track to the clubhouse, you may disagree.

North Cape Golf Club

LAKSELV, NORWAY – THE WORLD'S MOST NORTHERLY COURSE

NORTH CAPE IS THE WORLD'S most northerly golf club. At latitude 70, 300 miles (483km) inside the Arctic Circle, to get here you must take at least three flights – first to Norway's capital Oslo, then across the Arctic Circle to Tromso and then on to the world's most northerly airport at the small fishing town of Lakselv. From here it is a 25-mile (40km) journey to the course.

It is fair to say that your efforts in getting to North Cape will not be rewarded by a round on a majestic golf course. There are only six holes, two par-4s and four par-3s. The first hole, a par-4, is driveable. The second, the course's other par-4, is a drive and a pitch. The holes occupy two long fields which were given to the locals by a farmer. The clubhouse is a portacabin, and a few red chairs sit outside on a makeshift patio. Augusta it is not.

Nevertheless, the local townsfolk could not be more proud of their club. There is no greenkeeper, so the locals volunteer to mow the fairways and greens and help with the general upkeep of the club. The bunkers have been gouged out by diggers and are therefore invariably rectangular and shallow. On each tee there is a small, hand-painted map of the hole to come.

There are not too many hazards on the course, and even a drive hit into one of the gardens that border it is not considered out of bounds. Robin Sieger, who runs the Awesome Eight Challenge, did just that during his round here. "My playing partners told me to just walk into the garden and pitch back to the course," he recalls. "So I did. There was no wall or fence to climb. There is no sense of territory amongst Arctic Circle Norwegians."

But while you won't be overly challenged by the course, North Cape can offer you the curious experience of playing golf through the night. Although the course is open for only four months of the year, golf is nevertheless on tap here 24 hours a day from 17 May until 27 August. During these months the sun still sets, but hovers just below the horizon for around three hours.

Midnight golf at North Cape is ethereal. Usually a fine mist comes down and settles 3 feet (0.9m) or so from the ground. Look across the course and you will see only the top halves of golfers, swinging away at the vapour.

The course itself may be on the mundane side, but there is nothing ordinary about the scenery. Snowy mountains and glacier-gouged fjords flank the holes. The one drawback is the huge Arctic mosquitoes that plague the visiting golfer during the summer months. "You can hear them whirring through the air like Chinook helicopters," says Sieger. "If you don't watch out they will take a fair chunk out of your arm."

▼ *Midnight golf at North Cape Golf Club is a curious experience. Mist hovers 3 feet (0.9m) above ground.*

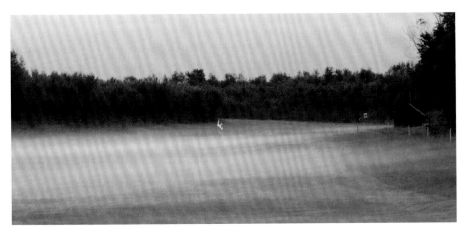

North Star Golf Club

FAIRBANKS, ALASKA – THE COLDEST COURSE ON EARTH

WHEN COURSE ARCHITECTS Jack Stallings and Hawley Evans laid out the holes for North Star Golf Club, Alaska, in 1991, they designed a fairly flat 8th green. Today it resembles a graveyard for beluga whales. That's what happens when you build a course on permafrost.

Welcome to the coldest golf club in the world. North Star is just outside Fairbanks, Alaska's second city after Anchorage. It is 200 miles (322km) south of the Arctic Circle, in the central eastern part of the state known as the "Interior". The lowest temperature ever recorded here is −52°C (-62°F). The average December temperature is a frostbiting -26°C (-79°F), and the course averages 10 inches (25cm) of snow each month from October to February. Wind chill is a major factor, and a 20mph (32kph) wind makes it feel even colder.

The permafrost underneath North Star's 18 holes creates an ever-changing arrangement of humps, swales and potholes. The course would look like a Scottish links were it not for the vivid wild Alaskan fireweed and the Canadian-looking blanket of black spruce trees covering the horizon. The course can only open for four months of the year – from mid-May to the end of September – and when the course starts to thaw in April, the staff reseed the course and overlay it with solar covers.

The hardy members of North Star play their golf in the knowledge that the ground could collapse at any moment. The area the course sits on was cleared for homesteaders in 1915, and that meant removing an insulating layer of moss. The ice was suddenly able to thaw much deeper, leaving underground voids that collapse at random, creating pits known as sinkholes.

Although summer conditions are often perfect for golf, temperatures can suddenly plunge to freezing. The best time to play here is around the midsummer solstice in June. The course is far enough north to offer midnight golf, and runs a 24-hour golf competition.

Playing at North Star can make you feel small. All around you is the vastness of nature, and it takes a massive state like Alaska – so big you could fit the whole of Europe into it – to accommodate it. But that's summer. When winter comes, the cold closes in. "Distances suddenly seem more imposing," says Roger Evans, the course's superintendent, architect, engineer, head caddie, bottle washer and spiritual guardian. "You start to realize that you won't make it far without a warm house in your near future. For us golfers, it's a case of sitting tight and waiting for the thaw."

Not so for member Dick Klapstein, who has taken to braving the snow for a few holes in winter-time. He has even invented a yarn "tail" for the ball to help him find it in the snow. "I tend to try and avoid the greens," he says, "but last time I played, there were a bunch of kids on snow machines going right over them."

North Star is perhaps the only course that sends you out with two scorecards. On one you mark down your score; on the other is a list of the wildlife you are likely to see during the round, and you are invited to tick them off as you see them. Red foxes, grizzly bears, wolves, eagles, owls, red-backed voles and moose are regular visitors. There is even a squirrel, infamous for stealing golf balls. If you are really lucky you may catch sight of a lynx, which is seen from time to time trying to catch local ducks.

The midnight golf experience is enhanced by the sight of moose. "They are used to the golfers," says Evans, "but you are best off leaving them alone. Like any animal they can get quite fierce if they feel threatened. At some stage during the round you will find yourself having to drop your ball from a moose hoofprint. Golf here is not about the perfect condition of the course, but about companionship. Or midnight solitude, if you prefer."

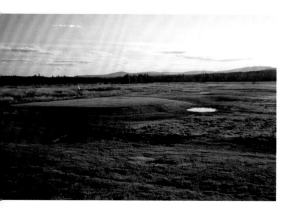

◀ *Extreme weather dictates that North Star Golf Club can only open from May to September, once the snow has thawed.*

Fajara Golf Club

FAJARA, GAMBIA – TOUGH GOING ON AFRICA'S WEST COAST

GOLFERS WHO ARE QUICK to make an excuse of a poor lie should play a round or two at the Fajara club, Gambia's only full-length golf course. Fajara's 18 holes run up, down and across the unkempt dunes on the west coast of this lozenge-shaped country, and good lies on the par-69 6,343-yard (5,800m) track come around like solar eclipses. Tees are sand pits, marked out by wooden boards. Greens, or rather browns, are fashioned from a crude concoction of sand and oil. Fairways are inundated with palm trees (which the greenkeeper is under strict instructions not to cut down) and run over rough sand, or at least they do for half a year. From June to October (Gambia's rainy season) the grass starts growing and the course turns from brown to green. This only makes things worse, however.

"When the grass comes it is not strong enough to support the weight of the ball," say Peter Videbe, a former treasurer at the club and a man who has worked tirelessly yet fruitlessly to promote golf in the Gambia. "So the ball nestles down. The other problem we have here at Fajara is fuel for the mowers. Very often there isn't any, so the grass grows and grows. It becomes harder and harder to find your ball."

The grass brings further problems. The course suddenly becomes a perfect grazing pasture, and local herders and their cattle make a beeline for the fairways. It is very common to see cows wandering the links. "We also get plenty of goats," adds Videbe. "And what the cows don't eat, the goats will. It is an ongoing battle to keep them off the course."

Sadly for Videbe and for Fajara, all efforts at training the cows and goats to chomp the grass in 20-yard (18m) strips down the marked fairways have so far proved ineffective. The resulting erratic lies make finding your ball an iffy business. And even if you do manage it, chances are it is lying in a hoof print.

Each group that plays Fajara goes out with a brownsweeper, a young caddie whose job it is to prepare the browns with diligent brooming. Paid 25 dalasis, about US$1, for his efforts, he is supposed to sweep the whole green for you, but sometimes the lads get lazy and just brush up your line to the hole. It sometimes pays to tip the brown-sweeper well. They are adept at putting small grooves into the browns with their brooms, which can help your ball track straight into the hole.

The front nine of the course is very hilly, while the back nine is a lot flatter. Its signature hole is the 13th, known as "Devil's Island", which is 394 yards (360m) long and features an island green. There are three water hazards on the course, at the 11th, 13th and 16th, and you can see the sea from most holes on the front nine. Temperatures average around 28˚C (82˚F), but can get up to 40˚C (104˚F) in the early afternoon. The course is a birdspotter's paradise, with 400 species visiting every year. Most common is the Abyssinian Roller, a spectacular bird with a stunning blue hue. Much harder to spot are the snakes; if you want to find boas, cobras, black mamba and vipers you can, but they will all hide from you. Most golfers are happy merely to see their tracks in the sand.

The Fajara Club is an old colonial course, built by the British with records dating back from 1937. It has billiards, tennis and squash as well as golf, and has around 300 members. About 60 play golf, half of which are Gambian and half British. "There are just three criteria for membership," says Videbe. "First, you must have some sort of residency in Gambia. Second, you must be able to pay the fee, which is around US$200. Third, no existing member of the club must hate you. This is very rare; in fact I can only think of one time this happened, when we kicked out an obnoxious tennis pro who tried to join."

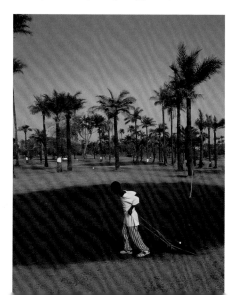

◀ *Young caddies are paid around 25 dalasis (about US$1) to sweep the browns for your group during your round.*

Gazetteer

Y

HOW TO CONTACT THE COURSES AND EVENTS FEATURED IN THIS BOOK

Courses

ALICE SPRINGS GOLF CLUB
Cromwell Drive, PO Box 2102, Alice Springs, Northern Territory, Australia 0871
Telephone: 61-8 8952 1921
Fax: 61-8 8953 4091
Website: www.alicespringsgolfclub.com.au
Email: asgc@alicespringsgolfclub.com.au

CYPRESS POINT GOLF CLUB
17 Mile Dr and Portolla, Pebble Beach, California 93953, USA
Telephone: 1-831 624 6444
Fax: 1-831 624 5057

COEUR D'ALENE RESORT
115 S. 2nd Street, PO Box 7200, Coeur d'Alene, Idaho 83816, USA
Telephone:1-208 765 4000
Fax: 1-208 664 7276
Website: www.cdaresort.com
Email: resortinfo@cdaresort.com

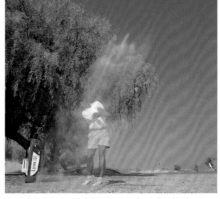

▲ *Dubai Country Club has plenty of grassless bunkers. Golfers carry a plastic "grass" mat around with them.*

CROSSE-GOLF ASSOCIATION
Maubeuge Place Town Hall, 59600 Maubeuge, France
Telephone: 33-327 64 10 47
Fax: 33-327 53 75 00

DUBAI COUNTRY CLUB
PO Box 5103, Dubai, United Arab Emirates
Telephone: 971-4 333 1155
Fax: 971-4 333 1409
Website: www.dubaicountryclub.com
Email: dcc@emirates.net.ae

EMIRATES CLUB, MAJLIS COURSE
PO Box 23, Ras Al Khaimah, United Arab Emirates
Telephone: 971-4 380 2222
Fax: 971-4 380 1555
Website: www.dubaigolf.com
Email: EGC@dubaigolf.com

FAJARA GOLF CLUB
Fajara, Kombo North, The Gambia, Africa
Telephone: 0207 376 0093 (Gambia National Tourist Office)
Fax: 0207 938 3644 (Gambia National Tourist Office)
Email: fajara@smiles.gm

FURNACE CREEK RESORT
Highway 190, Death Valley, California 92328, USA
Telephone: 1-760 786 2345
Fax: 1-760 786 2514
Website: www.furnacecreekresort.com
Email: info-fc@xanterra.com

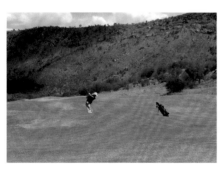

◄ *Alice Springs Golf Club, Australia, is the hottest course on earth with temperatures soaring to 50˚C (122˚F).*

HANS MERENSKY COUNTRY CLUB
Club Road, Phalaborwa, 1390, South Africa
Telephone: 27-15 781 3931
Fax: 27-15 781 5309
Website: www.hansmerensky.com
Email: gitw@hansmerensky.com

THE HIMALAYAN CLUB
Pokhara, West Nepal, Nepal
Telephone: 977-6127204
Fax: 977-61 21882
Website: www.travelnepal.com/adventure/golf
Email: himalaya@golf.mos.com.np

THE INTERNATIONAL GOLF CLUB
159 Ballville Road, Bolton, Massachusetts 01740-1227, USA
Telephone: 1-978 779 6919
Fax: 1-978 779 0231
Website: www.theinternational.com
Email: kathleen.kelly@theinternational.com

KABUL GOLF AND COUNTRY CLUB
Qargha Lake Golf Club, Qargha District, Northwest Kabul, Afghanistan
No contact details for the course are available. For information on the redevelopment of Afghanistan visit www.afghanistangov.org

KIAWAH ISLAND, OCEAN COURSE
12 Kiawah Beach Drive, Kiawah Island, South Carolina 29455, USA
Telephone: 1-843 768 2121
Fax: 1-843 768 6099
Website: www.kiawahgolf.com
Email: reservations@kiawahresort.com

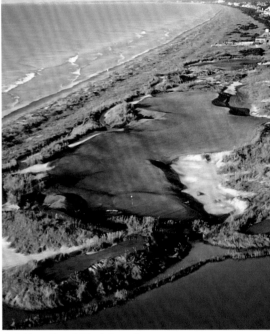

▲ *Golfers at Kiawah Island, Ocean Course, must negotiate lagoons, lakes and marshland during their round.*

KO'OLAU GOLF CLUB
45-550 Kionaole Road, Kane'ohe, Oahu, Hawaii 96744, USA
Telephone: 1-808 236 4653
Fax: 1-808 235 8295
Website: www.koolaugolfclub.com
Email: koolau@americangolf.com

LA PAZ GOLF CLUB
Casilla 4306, La Paz, Bolivia
Telephone: 591-2 274 5124
Fax: 591-2 274 5872
Website: www.lapazgolfclub.com
Email: infogolf@lapazgolfclub.com

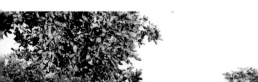

◀ *A 4X4 jeep at Hans Merensky Country Club in South Africa appears at dawn to sweep the course of any wildlife.*

Lost City Course, Sun City

Sun City Resort, PO Box 2, Sun City 0316, North West
Province, South Africa
Telephone: 27-14 557 1245
Fax: 27-14 657 3711
Website: www.suninternational.com/resorts/suncity/
Email: intmrk@sunint.co.za

Lucifer's Anvil Golf Course

19 Dana Point Road, Chico, California 95928, USA
Telephone: 1-530 892 2883
Fax: 1-530 892 8275
Website: www.keisterphoto.com
Email: doug@keisterphoto.com

The Machrie Hotel and Golf Links

Port Ellen, Isle of Islay, Argyll, Scotland PA42 7AN
Telephone: 44-1496 302310
Fax: 44-1496 302404
Website: www.machrie.com
Email: machrie@machrie.com

Macon la Salle Golf Club

71 260 La Salle, Burgundy, France
Telephone: 33-3 85 36 09 71
Fax: 33-3 85 36 06 70
Website: www.golfmacon.com
Email: golf.maconlasalle@wanadoo.fr

North Cape Golf Club

Postboks 98, 9711 Lakselv, Norway
Telephone: 47-78 462 376
Fax: 47-78 46 23 76
Website: www.northcape-golfclub.no
Email: post@northcape-golfclub.no

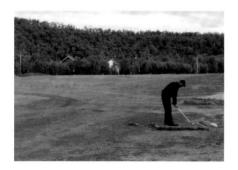

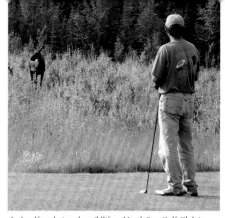

▲ *A golfer admires the wildlife at North Star Golf Club in
Alaska. The course is only playable for four months of the year.*

North Star Golf Club

330 Golf Club Drive, c/o Box 81090, Fairbanks, Alaska
99708, USA
Telephone: 1-907 457 4653
Fax: 1-907 457 3945
Website: www.northstargolf.com
Email:northstargolf@hotmail.com

Old Works Golf Course

1205 Pizzini Way, PO Box 100, Anaconda, Montana
59711, USA
Telephone: 1-406 563 5989
Fax: 1-406 563 3033
Website: www.oldworks.org
Email: mngr-professional@oldworks.org

Rotorua Golf Club

Arikikapakapa, Fenton Street, PO Box 6026, Rotorua,
New Zealand
Telephone: 64-7 348 4051
Fax: 64-7 348 1384
Website: www.rotoruagolfclub.co.nz
Email: rotorua@rotoruagolfclub.co.nz

St Andrews Old Course

St Andrews Links Trust, Pilmour House, St Andrews
KY16 9SF, Scotland
Telephone: 44-1334 466666
Fax: 44 1334 477036
Website: www.standrews.org.uk
Email: linkstrust@standrews.org.uk

◄ *Watch out for the huge arctic mosquitoes at North Cape,
Norway, the world's most northerly course.*

STONE CANYON CLUB
945 West Vistoso Highlands Drive, Oro Valley, Arizona
85737, USA
Telephone: 1-520 219 9000
Fax: 1-520 219 8000
Website: www.stonecanyon.com
Email: todd@stonecanyon.com

TPC AT SAWGRASS, STADIUM COURSE
110 TPC Drive, Ponte Vedra Beach, Florida 32082, USA
Telephone: 1-904 273 3235
Fax: 1-904 285 7970
Website: www.tpc.com/daily/sawgrass

USHUAIA GOLF CLUB
The Argentine Falklands 20 (9410), Ushuaia, Argentina
Telephone: 54-2901 432946
Fax: 54-2901 432946
Website: www.tierradelfuego.org.ar
Email: info@tierradelfuego.org.ar

THE VOLCANO GOLF AND COUNTRY CLUB
Pii Mauna Drive, Hawaii Volcanoes National Park,
Hawaii 96718, USA
Telephone: 1-808 967 7331
Fax: 1-808 985 8891
Website: www.volcanogolfshop.com
Email: support@volcanogolfshop.com

THE WAIKOLOA RESORT
600 Waikoloa Beach Drive Waikoloa, Hawaii 96738, USA
Telephone: 1-808 886 7888
Fax: 1-808 886 6546
Website: www.waikoloagolf.com
Email: golf@waikoloaland.com

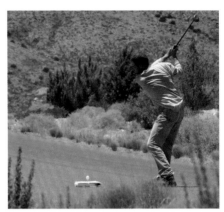

▲ *A competitor playing down the mountain at The Elfego Baca Shoot in New Mexico. The course has just one hole.*

Events

AWESOME EIGHT GOLF CHALLENGE
Telephone: 44-20 8875 8890
Website: www.awesomeeight.com
Email: info@awesomeeight.com

ELFEGO BACA SHOOT
Socorro Peak, Socorro, New Mexico, USA
Telephone: 1-505 835 8211
Website: www.hiltonopen.com
Email: hiltonopen@hiltonopen.com

THE UX OPEN
UXGA Tour Properties, LLC 107 Post Road East,
Westport, Connecticut 06880, USA
Telephone: 1-203 255 2891
Website: www.uxopen.com
Email: dkelly@uxopen.com

THE WORLD ICE GOLF CHAMPIONSHIP
P.O. Box 202, DK-3961 Uummannaq, Greenland
Telephone: 299-95 15 18
Fax: 299-95 12 62
Website: www.greenland-guide.gl/icegolf/
Email: icegolf@golfonice.com

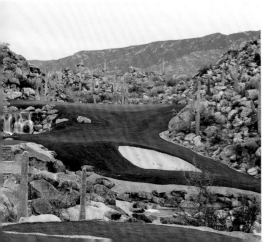

◀ *Stone Canyon Club, in Arizona, USA, is deep in the Sonoran desert. Saguaro cacti characterize the course.*

Index

🏌

Picture
Acknowledgements

The publisher wishes to thank the organisations and individuals listed below for their kind permission to reproduce the photographs in this book. Every effort has been made to acknowledge the pictures, however we apologise if there are any unintentional omissions.

B = bottom; L = left; R = right; T = top.

Front Cover: Drambuie World Ice Golf Championship Back Cover: Douglas Keister/www.keisterphoto.com 1 Tony Roberts Photography; 2–3 Douglas Keister /www.keisterphoto.com; 8–9 Phil Sheldon Golf Picture Library; 10 Dale Concannon Collection/Phil Sheldon; 12–13 Brian Morgan Golf Photography; 14–15 Robin Sieger; 16–17 Evan Schiller; 18–19 Chris Duthie; 20T Robin Sieger; 20B Robin Sieger; 21 Chris Duthie; 22–23 Brian Morgan Golf Photography; 23R Robin Sieger; 24–27 Action Images/David Slater; 28–29 Bob Krist/Corbis; 30–31 Furnace Creek Golf Course, Death Valley, CA; 31B Robin Sieger; 32–33 Rolling Greens Photo/Ken E May; 34–35 Barry Skipsey/Desert Express; 36–37 Robin Sieger; 38–39 Douglas Keister /www.keisterphoto.com; 40–45 Drambuie World Ice Golf Championship; 46–51 Douglas Keister /www.keisterphoto.com; 52 Dubai Country Club; 54–55 Phil Sheldon Golf Picture Library; 56–57 Graeme Matthews/PhotoNewZealand.com; 58T Graeme Matthews/PhotoNewZealand.com; 58B Tony Roberts Photography; 60–61 Tony Roberts Photography; 62–65 Richard Ansett; 67–69 UXGA Tour Properties, LLC; 70–71 Tony Roberts/Corbis; 72 Ian Jones/The Telegraph; 73 Julian Andrews/Rex; 74–75 Liz Anthony /Phil Sheldon; 77–79 Hans Merensky Hotel & Golf Estate; 80 Ann Cecil; 82 Evan Schiller; 83 Robin Sieger; 84–85 Ann Cecil; 86 Tony Roberts/Corbis; 88–89 Galen Rowell/Corbis; 90T J. D. Griggs – 2004; 90–91 Ann Cecil; 92–93 Nik Wheeler/Corbis; 94 Phil Sheldon Golf Picture Library; 95 Duif de Toit/Touchline Photo; 96 Rolling Greens Photo/Ken E May; 97 Buddy Mays /Travel Stock Photography; 98–99 Bob Krist/Corbis; 100–101 Tony Roberts/Corbis; 102 Tony Roberts /Corbis; 104–105 The Stone Canyon Club; 106 Evan Schiller; 108 Phil Sheldon Golf Picture Library; 109 Rolling Greens Photo/Ken E May; 110–111 Evan Schiller; 113–115 Michael Carroll 2003; 116–117 Empics; 118–119 Matthew Harris/The Golf Picture Library; 120 Dubai Golf Holidays + Events; 122–125 Aidan Bradley; 126–127 Phil Sheldon Golf Picture Library; 127B Allsport/Still Moving; 128 Tony Roberts Photography; 129 Tony Roberts /Corbis; 130 Tony Roberts Photography; 131 Tony Roberts/Corbis; 132–133 The Stone Canyon Club; 134–136 Peter Wong Photography; 137–139 The Stone Canyon Club; 141 archigolf-robert berthet; 142–143 Richard Ansett; 144–147 Joel Riner/ Quicksilver Studios; 148 Tony Roberts Photography; 149 Hilton Open Tournament Committee; 150 Himalayan Golf Course; 151 Robin Sieger; 152 Chris Duthie; 153 Allan Watson/Phil Sheldon; 154T Dubai Country Club; 154B Robin Sieger; 155T Kiawah Island Golf Resort; 155B Hans Merensky Hotel & Golf Estate; 156T Rogar Evans; 156B Robin Sieger; 157T Joe Warren/El Defensor Chieftan; 157B The Stone Canyon Club